Microstrategy Magic

Microstrategy Magic

Confronting Classroom Challenges While Saving Time and Energy

Michael S. Gaskell

ROWMAN & LITTLEFIELD
Lanham • Boulder • New York • London

Published by Rowman & Littlefield
An imprint of The Rowman & Littlefield Publishing Group, Inc.
4501 Forbes Boulevard, Suite 200, Lanham, Maryland 20706
www.rowman.com

6 Tinworth Street, London SE11 5AL, United Kingdom

Copyright © 2020 by The Rowman & Littlefield Publishing Group, Inc.

All rights reserved. No part of this book may be reproduced in any form or by any electronic or mechanical means, including information storage and retrieval systems, without written permission from the publisher, except by a reviewer who may quote passages in a review.

British Library Cataloguing in Publication Information Available

Library of Congress Cataloging-in-Publication Data

Names: Gaskell, Michael S, 1970- author.
Title: Microstrategy magic : confronting classroom challenges while saving time and energy / Michael S Gaskell.
Description: Lanham : Rowman & Littlefield, [2020] | Includes bibliographical references and index. | Summary: "Educators today must manage the constant disruptions that exist in a demanding, instant gratification world. This text provides solutions for dealing with time-consuming, exhausting challenges. Equipped with the tools to respond to these in an efficient manner, educators can get back to work helping students learn and grow into successful adults"—Provided by publisher.
Identifiers: LCCN 2020011293 (print) | LCCN 2020011294 (ebook) | ISBN 9781475855302 (cloth) | ISBN 9781475855319 (paperback) | ISBN 9781475855326 (epub)
Subjects: LCSH: Classroom management. | Time management. | Behavior modification.
Classification: LCC LB3013 .G376 2020 (print) | LCC LB3013 (ebook) | DDC 371.102/4—dc23
LC record available at https://lccn.loc.gov/2020011293
LC ebook record available at https://lccn.loc.gov/2020011294

I would like to dedicate this book to my wife, Michele, who possesses a beauty, love, and patience that makes her capable of accomplishing so much. She has inspired me with her work-life balance and her ability to be a strong female leader in her profession, an incredible mother, and a loving and dedicated wife. Without Michele, I could not have brought a dream like this book to reality, in a way that I hope helps so many others. Thank you Michele, for all of you have done.

Contents

Foreword	ix
Preface	xi
Introduction	xv
1 The Quick-Chat Intervention	1
2 There's More Power in Persuasion Than Push	9
3 The One-Liners That Disarm Any Parent, Student, or Others in Difficult Situations	21
4 Applying the Rule of 9s to Approach Every Challenge with Success	35
5 Taking on Test Anxiety with Three Simple, Effective Strategies	45
6 The Smartest Educators Steal	53
7 The Importance of the 80/20 Principle of Management	63
8 Getting Your School/Classroom to Perform Its Best in "Flow"	77
9 How to Know If It's All Working or Not, and What to Do about It: Engaging Parents: Embracing Diversity	89
10 Utilizing Nonfaculty Adults to Improve Your School Culture: How to Cut Your Bus Disciplinary Referrals by Two-Thirds	99
Appendix A: Faculty Biannual PLC Survey	109
Appendix B: Restorative Service Program Guidebook	115
Appendix C: Sample Communication Template	127
Bibliography	129

| Index | 131 |
| About the Author | 137 |

Foreword

As an administrator, time becomes your enemy. You make a list of things to do for the day, and on some days you are lucky to get one thing accomplished. The minute you walk into your building, there is a list of things for you to do, parents are waiting to see you, the bus driver is with kids who were brought to the office for misbehaving on the bus, teachers have a quick question to ask you, and there is a list of phone calls for you to make. Goodbye list of things to do—there are other priorities that now require your attention.

Dr. Gaskell has learned how to master challenges that bog practitioners down and distract them from putting their most important energy into helping children. He has put together strategies that are simple, low cost, and easy to replicate so practitioners can refocus their time and yet address the situation. Who isn't in favor of being able to use microstrategies to get through a challenge? I wish I had this book when I was starting out.

As an administrator with experience as a vice principal, principal, assistant superintendent, superintendent, and executive director for comprehensive supports and improvement at the New Jersey Department of Education working with low-performing schools and schools with an achievement gap, I have decades of experience at all levels, and I feel this book is a must-have for any practitioner. So when you have challenges such as being posed with the question *Are you calling my kid a liar?* or bus disciplinary problems, cafeteria worker situations, confrontational conversations, parents refusing to sign school documents, students with test anxiety, defusing difficult situations, or dealing with social media, strategies are right here at your fingertips to address the situation. How handy is that? I recommend this book to be in every practitioner's top desk drawer for a quick reference.

I have had the opportunity to see Dr. Gaskell in action as a colleague and through my work at the Department of Education. He has shared his strategies with colleagues via articles he wrote in 2018 and now has taken it to the next level with this book.

I recommend *Microstrategy Magic: Confronting Classroom Challenges While Saving Time and Energy* highly.

Dr. Mario C. Barbiere
educational consultant and author

Preface

Educators today face an increasing number of intensifying demands and less time to manage them. Finding effective ways to manage these often unexpected demands serves as a high-value commodity to expand the time to teach our ultimate goal: maximizing student success. I began writing articles in 2018 about some of the bigger challenges we face and how to overcome them or, more accurately, flip the script. I discovered that many readers were interested in these ideas: small, powerful strategies that work in effective, efficient ways.

It became evident that, like me, many educators were eager to grab hold of ideas that offered these kinds of options. If I could achieve so much more in my busy day by exercising these fast-acting and effective methods to address challenges, I could be a better educator, leader, and model to students and staff. The idea is to implement simple, sensible strategies that can and should be shared, just as I have borrowed from many others who have learned through their own experiences—specifically, how to master the challenges that bog us all down and distract us from putting our most focused energy into helping children.

Early in my writing, I felt the positive altruistic sensation of giving back to the education community, and it is this sensation that prompted me to write this book. It is my hope that you will come away from it with new, effective ideas to implement and to share with others. Even better, I'm hopeful you can take some of these ideas and expand and refine them into new and improved versions of the original!

Modern access to media offers the opportunity to network and share ideas in more immediate, accessible, and frequent ways. This book presents that opportunity. The strategies advanced are intentionally simple, low cost, and able to be immediately replicated and implemented just about anywhere and anytime. They are the product of learned methods from a collection of more than two decades of experience and the wise decision to borrow from others and refine those ideas where evidence of repeated success has been demonstrated.

These experiences include my own childhood struggles, methods learned from my work as a special educator, and my more recent experiences as an administrator. Yet the best come from those in the trenches every day, from those master teachers I continue to watch in awe, wondering, *How did they do that?* Some are a combination of all of these. To me, the best part is that they are easily transferrable and immediately dispensable, offering a way out of situations that may otherwise be daunting, detrimental, or—worse—impossible to overcome.

As you read and discover the ideas offered in this text, I would like to stress that the goal of this book is very personal to me. These strategies have been proven valuable through dozens of workshops and articles. When I was a young student, my mother saw signs that I was struggling academically, socially, and developmentally, and she requested an evaluation to be conducted by the school psychologist. Here are some of the conclusions from the school psychologist's report:

- ability in the below-average, slow-learner intelligence range
- depressed scores in the verbal area
- social awareness and social interactions—significantly depressed, suggesting a problem with social skills
- academic achievement approximately six months below grade level
- has hostility and poor impulse control, which surfaces in socially inappropriate ways
- is negative toward school; feels unable to succeed academically

I share these very personal and challenging conclusions about my young life as an important message that, writing to you as an educational leader, I know it's possible to help any child under any circumstance—including the most overwhelming and formidable circumstances—to excel and become the best version of themselves. This is made possible through microstrategies, a collection of quick, effective methods to help enhance a positive school climate, build a first-rate faculty, effectively foster relations with parents and community members, and most importantly, help students improve and believe in themselves.

I would like to thank my mother for believing in me when the writing on the wall suggested otherwise, my wife and children for being supportive, and all the children out there who showed me how an underdog can overcome any obstacle.

Finally, it is important to emphasize that this book is divided in a way to enable its use as reference tool that can be looked back on in sections and repeatedly referred to for its enduring strategy implementation. This is because the microstrategies offered within each section offer short, simple techniques written in practical language. Like the concepts in the book, the ideas are subdivided for fast, applicable, and immediately replicable benefit to the reader. You can refer to them at any time, either in a weekend reading or by indexing them for easy access when you need that one strategy to get you through a challenge.

Introduction

It was a typical winter day and teachers were seated around a table in the faculty lounge, sipping coffee in a vain attempt to reenergize, venting about the challenges of dealing with disrespectful students, lawnmower parents, and unsupportive administrators. This could be any suburban middle school America, with a group gathered during their typically brief lunch period, depleted, and caught in the crosshairs of repeatedly frustrating cycles.

The teachers had just heard the news about a student's physical assault on a teacher. What was worse, they noted, was that this child had a modified behavior plan that apparently prevented him from being held accountable for such appalling, frightening behavior. While this is not something most educators would characterize as a "typical" occurrence on a given school day, incidences of alarming behaviors such as this appear to be increasing.

Many possibilities may reveal why this is so. It could be the recognition of trauma in students' lives, difficult parents, the emotional impact of social media, or the increase of at-risk students entering schools from at-risk homes. The reality is that some or all these factors—and many others—are the cause of the increasingly frequent occurrence of alarming student behaviors.

Recognizing and anticipating that these challenges exist in schools today, we can be better equipped to manage them, be it with students themselves, their parents, or the reactions of our colleagues. The most effective strategies must be quick—or, as I refer to them, "micro"—and they must be replicable across our schools. That is not to say that every microstrategy works in every circumstance with every child. Rather, some of these will work in some circumstances, which is far better than the outcome where a student assaults a teacher, or faculty turns toxic because they feel helpless, or student achievement decreases as a result of the poor school climate.

These microstrategies are time-tested and have been utilized by the greatest skeptics, who frequently turned into the best salespeople for the idea. They have been effectively used with often surprising success at minimal cost of our most precious resource—time. As busy educators, with literally hundreds of interactions in a given day, we have no time to waste. Making efficient use of microstrategies allows educators to better utilize their time helping students perform at their best. In fact, the use of a strategy can go hand in hand with this standard.

This book is organized so that the miscrostrategies outlined offer the educator or aspiring educator to read in ways that answer those questions that without this resource, they would otherwise not have the answer for. These microstrategies can be pulled out in a variety of ways, like tools from a toolbox, and used to resolve specific conundrums. Whether readers use these strategies to attack an immediate problem or referring to the index to seek a solution to longstanding challenges, this book has achieved its purpose in helping the taxed educator resolve issues in surprisingly effective, and even energizing, ways.

The hope is that at this point your interest has been piqued enough to trigger you to ask, "So what kind of microstrategies are you talking about, and how can they really help me with my exhausting, time-consuming, and daunting problems?" How, you wonder (for instance), could I possibly address the issue of a student assaulting a teacher? Alternatively, it is possible you have already placed your finger on a section title that reflects your current predicament. Either way, it is worth your time to enjoy discovering these microstrategies, in part or whole, as you will come away from the reading armed with one or more new ideas or approaches to resolve your issue.

While teachers should never have to contend with an assault, there are proactive means one can enlist in order to prevent such traumatic experiences. Understand that I do not condone violence or any of the other adverse events addressed in this book as some of the most common trials faced by teachers and administrators within schools many times every day. Rather, I am acknowledging that these challenges exist and that it is our response to or anticipation of them that arms us with the power to shift problems into solutions and in our favor.

If you have come this far, perhaps you are willing to read just a little bit further to get a dose of a microstrategies. So let's explore one before offering an inventory of the others in the chapters ahead. We will examine how utilizing a microstrategy can positively impact our important work with children in time-sensitive and constructive ways.

The impact of trauma poses a substantial risk to students—something that is recognized now more than ever before. Increased reports of trauma and tragic circumstances resulting from trauma—such as increases in at-risk behaviors and even suicide—are bona fide challenges schools face today. How, then, can we proactively address issues like assault or other serious infractions in schools today?

WHEN YOU MOVE THE BODY, YOU MOVE THE MIND

We know from scientific research that movement is not only good for your body and physical health, it is also very important for your mind. In fact, it decreases depression, anxiety, sleep disturbance, and even post-traumatic stress disorder (PTSD). There are a couple of different ways to use this strategy. First, consider embracing a daily school-wide or class-wide morning routine, such as a three-minute meditation. While you may think this is not exercise, mindfulness activities have a profound impact on student physiology, enhancing both student wellness and achievement. This kind of mind and body activity can set the stage for a cascade of positive effects throughout a child's day.

The second way to look at this is in advance of a big test or standardized assessment. Have students follow along an exercise routine in the classroom—you can find examples on YouTube—and yes, these can be done in class. Better yet, have your physical education teacher make a video—students are likely to connect more to the teachers they know—and play energetic or motivational background music. Getting the body activated in this way is important, especially right before a long period of sitting, and it inspires a child's mind to think more creatively and critically.

If students are moving—and therefore moving their mind to think more logically—they will apply more logical decisions to the circumstances they face. A school learned this with a child who could become violent because he was driven to believe he had no other way to respond to his circumstances. Whether that was justified or not is irrelevant. It is how he felt.

Applying practical solutions, such as moving a child in advance of a long sedentary period—or better yet, at intermittent intervals throughout the day—is not only pragmatic, it is advisable. It's true that not every student will respond in the extreme, with violence. Yet even those who do not may apply more passive-aggressive responses to teacher direction. These are often more frustrating behaviors because they are more subtle and sustained.

Violence is extreme, and when it can be avoided, apply movement strategies, either as a school community or at a classroom level. Remember that this can be as simple as a two-minute stretch and stand, right at student seats. One school counselor walked around the building with a student who was on the verge of exploding, picking up trash around the school, and eventually the student followed by doing the same. This was both movement and contribution, something that places value on the subject.

During movement, add music to stimulate the auditory receptors, be it through distraction or instilling a sense of tranquility. Violence is one matter, yet more common and draining behaviors by students are those that wear even the most energized teachers down. Movement certainly offers these students, too, a way to get circulation moving and brain activity going. This will not solve every problem every time, but you would be surprised at how effectively this short burst of intermittent rejuvenation is. After all, if this microstrategy is used to prevent or minimize everything from assault to passive-aggressive behavior, isn't it worth a try?

As you read this text, know that the best ideas are borrowed and even modified. Happy reading; enjoy the book. Remember that microstrategies are fluid. They can be utilized individually or stacked as a group for the purpose of effectively countering the modern-day challenges we face. If you have your own ideas, it would be great to share these with our new community of microstrategy networked educators at: mikesmicrominute.com.

Chapter One

The Quick-Chat Intervention

INTRODUCING THE QUICK-CHAT INTERVENTION

One conversation, one brief chat, lasts moments—just seconds or perhaps minutes. It is these short bursts of time where delivery can have a profoundly positive or negative impact depending on your approach. This type of interaction is incredibly overlooked, and its power is easily misunderstood. Yet the right kind of chat can have an impact on a child that lasts days, or even a lifetime. Choosing how to engage in this chat is far more significant than we might consider in the fleeting moments of a busy school day. Consider the inspiring scenarios that follow.

All kids can benefit from the quick-chat intervention, especially those who are at the greatest risk. One such child who had been in quite a bit of trouble in middle school returned as an adult to speak to younger students about the influence of an adult on his life through conversations that built a support system that was not present in other areas of his life. Here is his story, as shared by his older self:

> At this time, I was failing every class except gym. The principal saw I was having a rough time and tried to help. Sometimes he would call me down just to spend one of my periods talking with him and he would give me a cup of hot chocolate when we were talking. He recognized that I was having a hard time and that I didn't feel heard, so he took time out of his work schedule to meet with me. He was my positive support at that time. Fast forward to tenth grade. At this time, things got worse at home. My mom was drinking alcohol every day. She started using drugs and bringing drug dealers into our home. Sometimes she would disappear for days, leaving my brother and me home alone to fend for ourselves. Many times, we didn't have food or clean clothes. My only safe place was school. At school, there were people who helped me get food, washed my clothes, and gave me guidance. I received a lot of positive supports

which helped me to strive for greater things. . . . I choose to focus on my achievements as I am about to head into college. If you may be a foster kid, or someone who gets into trouble, just know there are people that are rooting for you and want to see you succeed.

Another example involved a teacher who arrived at the school's main office, red-faced and with a student in tow, looking extremely agitated. As the principal greeted them both in a cheery voice, "Good morning!" the teacher announced, "This student"—pointing to her to be sure it was known to whom she was referring, though no other students were present in the main office—"told me that *you* said she could carry a backpack around in the halls!" If it were possible for steam to be coming out of her ears like a cartoon character at that very moment, this would have visibly matched her tone to all in the office.

The principal had never told any students that they could carry a backpack in the halls. As a middle school leader, he was concerned about too much weight being strapped on the backs of adolescents throughout a full school day, as children grow quickly and this pressure can certainly have negative consequences on their development. He was dumbfounded that such an obvious deception by a student would affect this teacher in such a striking way.

As a new principal, one of the challenges is to win over the informal powers in the building. The principal was still sizing up who those individuals were, and this teacher may likely have been one of them. (He later learned that, in fact, she was.) It would have been easy to fall prey to this teacher's expectation to scold this child with an angry, "I didn't tell her that! How dare you? You are in big trouble!"

But how would that have affected this child? Would she comply? Would she respect the authority figures in the building? What would this have taught her? And how would this teacher ever learn that this is no way to ever speak to a child, regardless of what she had done? The principal was still struggling to understand why this teacher believed a child making up that the principal told her it was okay to do something was criminal, given it was not a criminal offense.

The principal announced, "I will take it from here." The teacher stood motionless in disbelief, waiting for more. He repeated, "Thank you. I will take it from here." She hesitated, and then slowly walked out, backward, as if to show that she was keeping an eye on him. He was wondering if she would point toward her two eyes as she backed away. Then she pivoted and walked out triumphantly, waxing victorious for all to see in the hallway.

With the teacher removed, he looked more closely at the student, who appeared troubled by more than just agitation from this teacher encounter. This was a young lady he knew well. She was oppositional, combative, and noncompliant. She was seriously at risk, and she made life difficult for the faculty in the building. But there was something more.

He brought the student into his office and, ignoring the current issue, asked her, "What's wrong? You look worried about something." She looked at him with suspicious eyes, and after a hesitation, responded, "My mom didn't come home last night." He quickly responded, "Let me see if I can help you find your mom." He called her grandmother, the local police department, and a family friend listed on the emergency contact list, and in fifteen minutes was able to locate her mother.

As the student waited in the office area, where chairs lined a windowed wall as typical for a school, he came to her side and told her, "I found your mother. She's okay. Come, let's talk with her." An incredible sigh of relief visibly passed through her entire body, and the strain of a once-worried face that gave her the look of someone who just found out someone close to her had been in a terrible accident gave way to relief. He handed her the phone, and she spoke with her mother for a few minutes before saying goodbye.

On the other side of this early morning saga was an angry veteran teacher, ready to pounce on "the new principal who doesn't know how to hold kids responsible" with far greater informal power than he had yet earned from his faculty. But back to the student: As she awaited her "sentencing," he looked at her and said, "I'm really glad you don't have to worry about that now, and you can get on with your day. Oh, and by the way, about the backpack—"

He didn't even have to finish his sentence. This tough, streetwise kid arose from her chair, not as a challenge but rather as a sign of respect, and said with streetwise force, "Sir, I will never carry my backpack in the halls again, and I know I have to get suspended." He looked at her for a moment and replied, "Well, yes, there is some discipline involved, but I believe you, and I thank you for telling me you won't carry your backpack again."

It would be a fairy tale to say that the rest of this child's days at school were perfection—but that claim would be categorically false. She could present a challenge from day to day, but for the rest of her stay at that school, all the principal ever had to do was give her a look in the hall or pull her aside for a quick chat, and she complied. And the angry teacher? She asked him what in the world had he done to "scare" her into not carrying her backpack ever again!

This teacher was not yet ready for the truth. She wouldn't have believed him because she had too much pride to think otherwise. He just smiled and said, "I'm glad I was able to resolve this." It would be months before he could start teaching his faculty—and only after they had seen this in action, modeling the way that just one critical chat at the right moment could have far-reaching and powerful consequences for any child, no matter how challenged or at risk.

These stories illustrate how small moments, opportunities for a quick chat, can result in positive outcomes. Some had the potential to send a child down a destructive path of noncompliance or disrespect toward authority figures who applied disproportionate responses to student misbehavior. Our primal nature teaches us to react in this way. Tapping into higher thought processes in microdoses has far-reaching consequences for success within a school's culture and climate, and, just as importantly, in student achievement. Considering this perspective, which way will you respond the next time you face an encounter like this?

In the pages ahead, you will read more stories, some of which are about me, some about colleagues and those involved in athletic programs, and some about children. These children that I had the good fortune to teach and to learn from were either inspired or shut down, setting the stage for a chain of events that had a profound impact on their lives. In each of these is a lesson, a practical application focused on doable microstrategies you can apply to change your school, your classroom, or even one child for the better.

The quick-chat intervention doesn't just work with kids. This strategy works with teachers, colleagues, and parents. Children bring out the best in parents. They also bring out the worst. There are many times parents call a school demanding justice or action while missing many of the parts of a story or event.

It is important to remember that parents are reacting, whether in a reasonable or an emotionally charged and irrational way, because their children are precious to them. They love and adore their children. The best way to turn parents around is to get them to understand that you care about their children too. This sparks an immediate connection about something that matters more than pride. What follows is another quick-chat intervention that works 100 percent of the time.

YOUR KID, MY KID

Virtually every administrator and an increasing number of teachers have experienced a parent who emotionally charges in at them with part of a story, a grossly inaccurate account of an event characterized by their child, or their own emotional misperception. When this happens, it is only human nature to feel defensive.

Being defensive is also the least effective way to reach parents who are upset about something connected to their child. Instead, try a simple, quick strategy that works because it's a trust-building technique. After taking the time to listen carefully to the parent without interrupting, consider acknowledging the parent's concern. This is not agreement, but rather acceptance of their feelings.

Following an acknowledgement of concern, simply respond with the following: "I know that she is your child. However, I am going to be somewhat selfish for a moment. When she is at my school, she is my child, and I will treat her as my own." This statement, short and deliberate, also has the effect of tugging on parents' heartstrings in a way that a much more labor-intensive and often unproductive argument does not. It speaks volumes to the care you have for the child. It builds trust. It opens the door to working together. No longer does the parent feel defensive and ready for a fight; instead, he or she is open to working alongside you to help the child. After all, isn't that our objective? Isn't this how we want to reach parents, to successfully help work with their children?

Let's think about this objectively for a moment. We are attempting to get parents on our side. This is often a costly waste of our most valuable resource: time. By gaining parents' trust and belief in our personal stake in their child, we can eliminate or at least significantly reduce those challenges that bear the greatest burden on our work as educators. Indeed, we can prevent significant amounts of time being wasted having to explain the situation to our boss, adding a second uncomfortable discussion to the previous one. Time is something we never have enough of and we need to find ways to economize. It comes at a costly expense when dealing with social media misinformation too.

FIGHTING BACK AGAINST SOCIAL MEDIA MISINFORMATION

Looking forward to a quiet, peaceful Saturday, the last thing an educational leader wants is a cell phone lighting up about a social media frenzy going on about an incident at school. Having dealt with the incident the day prior, it is not uncommon for us to be shocked at the incredible inaccuracy detailed in a social media thread by those referring to it—or rather, grossly distorting a version that is so far from reality that one can find it unimaginable how it came to be.

In one example, a grossly inaccurate suggestion was bandied about social media that two students had brought guns to school and that they were arrested and sent to juvenile detention, or "juvy," as it was called in the Facebook posts by parents. The reality: a child had brought a letter opener to school and, when confronted by a peer, turned himself in to the office.

The mistake many school communities make is either to simply ignore the insanity of such social media inaccuracies or to send a letter home to parents offering a vague explanation in a weak attempt to address the gross rumors. The truth is that you must fight back against social media misinformation immediately and objectively, for two very important reasons:

- Telling the truth about an issue offers transparency to parents surrounded by social media misinformation, and transparency builds trust in a school community.
- If you respond properly to it, you can change the misinformation narrative.

This can be accomplished swiftly and save costly hours explaining in board meetings, in discussions with dozens of parents who call with concerns, or in the media. The simple formula involves engaging parents who personally trust and reach out to you. Every administrator knows this parent or group of parents. Use them as a vehicle. Do not go on social media and engage. That's where the online game of telephone perpetuates into a vicious cycle in which no educational leader should ever engage.

Instead, simply write (in an e-mail if possible) parents who can influence the conversation or tell them to post that they heard directly from you and that you requested they put a very simple statement in the thread. In the incident described above, this looks like a parent promoting the following for the principal:

> I spoke with the principal, and this is what he said: "The comments are incorrect. The fact is that one child brought in a letter opener and never revealed it to anyone. The letter opener was confiscated by the office and the child received appropriate disciplinary action. No child was in jeopardy at any time. Please feel free to copy and paste this entire message into your post."

In the incident described above, the thread immediately took a different direction. As a matter of fact, the administrator received praise for his transparency and for extinguishing rumors that were born of the online game of telephone. Comments like, "Finally, some honest effort at putting parents' minds at ease!" and, "Wow, straight from the horse's mouth! Now I can go back to work resting easy that my child is safe!"

This story quickly dissipated and parents expressed relief before moving on with their weekend. There was no board meeting with an armada of concerned parents, no news media inaccurately covering this story; the school resumed its day-to-day function and the staff were able to get back to what counts: helping children.

Another method to employ is to mirror your statement to the parent posting for you in an all-call, if such a system exists within your school community. This further reinforces that you are not afraid to confront the misinformation campaign and set things straight. This method has also been utilized effectively by a school in which parents and/or students were claiming that students opting out of standardized testing were being punished by having to sit in a room with no stimuli, while the others watched movies when testing was over. This was categorically false, and the principal tapped a respected, influential parent to set the record straight—and again, it quickly was.

CHAPTER SUMMARY

1. *Introducing the Quick-Chat Intervention.* This is most needed when it may seem hardest to do. Educators who are in a hurry, having to move on to the next of many important tasks, may lose sight of the need to stop, take a micromoment, and give children the attention or approach they need. In fact, this helps save time, and those engaging students in numerous interactions throughout the day would be wise to stop, listen, and respond in ways that effectively reverse destructive reactions by children.
2. *Your Kid, My Kid.* This shows parents that you care for their child above anything else. This helps to clear the air about your intentions without draining resources and time to convince them. Getting them to see this creates a bond that will help you move beyond the issue and on to more productive encounters with parents to help their child.
3. *Fighting Back against Social Media Misinformation.* This is important because of the power inaccurate information has to overtake the truth, especially on social media. Do not fear transparency; embrace it to extinguish falsehoods on social media. This will serve any educator well, as the school needs to write the true story of its many great accomplishments, not the false narrative that can dangerously spread like a virus on social media.

Chapter Two

There's More Power in Persuasion Than Push

A keynote speaker at an educational conference laid it all out with one simple yet global statement: "There's more power in persuasion than push." This was in the context of convincing a hardened faculty to try something new. He had tried to force compliance on his faculty and realized he was making both his and their lives miserable in the process. The truth is, you cannot force compliance and truly achieve the most desirable results. Yes, it's possible to mandate, but that works only if we're looking. The moment we turn our attention away, compliance stops and resistance swells.

It is also essential to recognize that whether forcing compliance or persuading an individual or group to make changes, we will likely never achieve 100 percent consensus. This is the reality of making changes or seeking buy-in on new ideas. Knowing this, why not go with the greater success rate? Wouldn't perhaps 85 percent consensus be better than 65 percent? Remember that improvement—not perfection—is the key to making successful change, getting an initiative off the ground, or seeking to accomplish any objective. Following, then, are some examples of ways to persuade those individuals in our charge enough to tip the balance in the direction of what we hope to achieve in our classrooms and schools, rather than trying to force buy-in.

THE $6 T-SHIRT

If you've ever been to a special event, a game, or even a fundraiser, you have likely observed an event organizer launching promotional T-shirts into the crowd. Everyone goes crazy, and as the T-shirts are tossed or shot out of a cannon, people jump up to grab them with energy and high levels of excitement. Why? Is this T-shirt a first edition made exclusively by Ralph Lauren? Certainly not. In fact, if you walked by this shirt in your local Walmart, you probably would not even notice it—or worse, you might wish that you could unsee it. But that's not why people want the shirt. There's something much more powerful going on here, and the logic behind it can be applied effectively as a microstrategy in your classroom or school.

A new teacher wanted the kids in his class to like him and respond to him positively. He felt obligated to offer the best incentives he could find. Little did he know what a big mistake that would turn out to be. Aside from being a just-out-of-college, loan-ridden newbie who could barely afford ramen noodles—let alone lofty awards for his new classroom-management system—he realized over time that the best incentives were low-cost or free because they actually worked far more effectively on the brains of students.

On one occasion, he convinced the class that if they accomplished their goals for the week, on Friday afternoon they would have a full class period to enjoy a party, watch a movie, or engage in a free-time activity of their choice. There were several significant mistakes in this approach. First, a forty-five-minute celebration became the expectation, not the special circumstance; this is something perhaps you may want to do at the end of a school year. And at what cost? Students lost considerable instructional time. Even worse, they quickly expected more, asking, "Why not have two class periods next time?" If you have ever observed twenty-five adolescents with forty-five minutes of unstructured time, you can appreciate the challenges of begging the clock to move a little faster toward 3:00 p.m.

First-year teachers do not have endless funds to "buy" kids into being well behaved, so this is not sustainable nor is it a way to teach cost value to children. A better way to motivate students is to transition from extrinsic to intrinsic motivation. A simple microstrategy is to encourage your students to be motivated by the little things and allow them to focus on the why of winning rather than the value of the prize. Effectively reinforced, small incentives are more desirable than big rewards.

Another advantage of low- or no-cost prizes (like two minutes of free time) is that you can offer them more frequently than a lavish grand prize. This is an invaluable injection into your school's culture dynamic during critical phases of the school year, often when it's most needed. This kind of infusion is ideal for reducing behavior issues that tend to accelerate in the excitement leading up to the week before the winter holiday.

If you have already started a resource- or incentive-heavy reward system, don't worry. Undoing costly resource-heavy rewards and incentives takes some time, but the longer-term payoffs are worth far more than the time it takes to unravel previous expectations. If you have been giving out big incentives in your classroom or school—or the reverse, none at all—this method is easy to switch to, it's replicable, and it works.

You can start at any time, but be patient: Transferring from extrinsic resource-heavy rewards to low- or no-cost incentives takes time. Using intrinsic rewards, the brain becomes a powerful resource to tap into. When students buy in, there's a positive energy and competitive spirit—and it certainly feels better than bargaining with kids over forty-five or ninety minutes of unstructured free time! Remember the concept of the $6 T-shirt. Consider the following list of examples; for a larger library of suggestions, see the website PBIS Rewards (Positive Behavior Interventions and Supports, www.pbisrewards.com).

> Fast pass on the lunch line
> Eat lunch with your choice of friends at a priority table with games, preferential seating, or other incentivized options to select from
> Homework pass
> Dollar store prize
> $5 school store gift certificate
> JibJab a teacher or friend

WHO DO YOU SIT CLOSER TO IN A DIFFICULT CONVERSATION BETWEEN TWO PEOPLE?

It can be a stressful experience to be faced with the inevitable encounter educators face regularly: sitting among a group of tense parties who are at opposing viewpoints over an issue. Our role as educators often requires us to be situated at meetings or in conferences with pairs of these parties. This could be a child study team meeting, a disciplinary meeting with administration and students or parents, or a meeting among colleagues where you may be confronted as a mediator. Unfortunately, this means that eventually we will all experience a meeting with two or more individuals where both sides are being difficult or are facing difficult situations.

In these cases, we may meet people who are inherently unpleasant or difficult, or they may be people facing a daunting circumstance that is causing them to act in a problematic way. Think about it like this: We have all faced a challenge that seemed overwhelming to us. We sometimes react in ways that were not the norm for us. The worst version of ourselves may be exposed, and that is no different than the difficult person.

Whether you are encountering a difficult person or a person in a difficult situation, it is important to remember the power of the brain and how to effectively but professionally stand your ground. The ground is both physical and mental ground. Proximity and presence are far more important than we may be consciously aware of. So who do you sit closer to in a meeting with difficult people? There's a simple microstrategy to apply in this situation: *Whoever is the most difficult!*

As unnatural as this may feel or sound, let's consider why: When people are in a difficult state of mind, they are tapping their primal instincts—fight or flight. Ego typically drives them to fight. In a professional setting, this is counterproductive because it aggravates the situation if both sides are in the fight mode. We need to draw them away from this and back to dialogue. If someone is physically distant from you, it is far easier for the person to mentally distance from you as well. In order to disrupt this powerful mental pattern, start by breaking down the physical barrier.

Consider this scenario: A difficult parent was known for being a bully. He threw his weight around, and worse, seemed to have little respect for women. The principal arrived a few minutes late at a scheduled meeting where this parent and a group of teachers were sitting. The principal's late arrival was intentional. The parent was visibly stretched out as if in a power pose, strategically seated away from cautious-looking and uncomfortable teachers. The principal squeezed a chair in between a counselor and this parent, but the parent did not shift, as one would naturally do to make room for an arriving person. So the principal squeezed in even further. The parent remained frozen and never made eye contact, as if to send an intimidating message of posturing.

Whether the parent scaled down his approach or not (he did in this scenario), equally powerful as getting him to back off was what the principal's intentional placement symbolized to the educators observing this in the room. She was not going to be intimidated by this person, physically or psychologically. Like teachers modeling for students, the principal sent an importantly message to her faculty: *We will work professionally with those meeting with us, but we will not be intimidated by them, at any time, at the cost of the children affected by this meeting.*

Other examples of this include a teacher or administrator sitting next to a parent or student, rather than behind the desk. These examples of proximity control permeate the school community and empower the faculty to be cordially up front in ways that break down obstacles to successful communication. By choosing to use proximity strategically, we can reduce the impediments to humanizing our work with others and get to the task of helping students in ways that save time and energy and prevent misunderstanding.

USE YOUR CELL PHONE

Unions are necessary support systems for educators, especially in a time where we more frequently risk being unfairly and inaccurately attacked. Educators should and must have certain protections in place. The collaboration between strong union leadership, the administration, and the community are critical components to this support system.

It is reasonable, then, to appreciate and value our support networks. These can include the union, mentors, coaches, or trusted old sages. Yet it is also reasonable to disagree with some of their guidance and support. Not all the right answers come from one direction. Considering professional discretion and flexibility about where your best ideas and strategies are borrowed from can add to your liberties as a caring professional and further reduce the obstacles that the appearance of bureaucracy often perpetuates.

One of the most common refrains new and inexperienced educators hear from their support systems is to *never* use your cell phone to communicate with families, the community, or even your boss. This is also one of the most misrepresented cautions about communication. Indeed, we live in a world where scam callers are bombarding our personal cell phone space. Why in the world, you might ask, would we want to add the risk of opening our personal space up more? Let us take a closer look at why the fear exists and what to consider when opening the lines of communication up via cell phone or other spaces.

The caution is typically presented from one of two perspectives. First, there is the fear that if you share communication through your personal cell phone, you are granting access to individuals not in your personal life and thus causing a clash between the professional and personal lines. There could be merit to this, given concerns about teacher wellness and the need to respect boundaries between the personal and the professional.

This fear suggests that you need to separate your communication for your own privacy and sanity. The second concern relates back to the support system educators have around them: a mentor, the union, or a colleague disenfranchised about a negative experience with a parent. These individuals may very well have good intentions. They caution their colleague to avoid breaking down these same professional and personal lines. This line of thinking considers the protections in place for educators to insulate themselves from the dark forces that exist beyond our classroom walls.

Really? Let's think about this for a moment. In the first of these two arguments, the breaking down of personal versus professional barriers, is actually a good argument for avoiding social media. Educators should be more cautious about sharing their personal information over social media, and many—often the same ones who wouldn't share their correspondence via cell phone—do not.

Yet what is so personal about a single back-and-forth communication via text or a call between cell phones? The only fear here is that your words could be shared on social media; therefore, you should only ever use your cell phone for good reasons, such as to help a person or child, and use professionally appropriate dialogue. This is a win-win because anything shared is a positive promotion on your behalf.

In the second argument, the need to insulate oneself truly rests with individuals making the decision to share their cell phone number. It is true that there are certain individuals interacting with educators with whom you should never, ever use your cell phone as a communication vehicle. This is not because of a fear that the cell phone will be shared or that the individuals will abuse their access, but rather simply for your own sanity. Difficult and unreasonable people exist in every educator's world, and these individuals do not deserve more direct access. But almost everyone else does and should.

If an educator truly regrets sharing access, remember that cell phones now possesses the technology to hit a button and block a number. Given the rule about never granting access to truly challenging individuals, one educator reports that in more than two decades of sharing access, he has never had to block a number and in fact has only once received a few text responses that came close to crossing the line. He simply ignored these texts and instead, the next time the individual who had texted him saw him the texter apologized. The educator said, "no problem," and never received another message by text again.

Keep in mind that using your cell phone should not be a regular occurrence. It always comes down to timing. There are two significant benefits to this for the educator. First, if it was a busy day and you just could not get to everything, a follow-up call to a parent, vendor, community member, or other person on the car ride home that evening is a great way to knock out something that would have been piled onto the next day's already frenetic schedule. Second, this is simply great public relations.

Let us examine the second benefit a little closer and observe how one educator seizes on this as a way to advertise a positive school-to-community relationship. As schedules were opening at the end of the summer for students, a typical issue surfaced: a child's schedule had an error on it. The child was already anxious about moving up to a new school, and this anxiety could be intensified by the confusion and unknown results of this error.

The child's parent called the counseling office on a Friday afternoon before the Labor Day weekend, when no one would be back until Tuesday. Seeing the concern, the counselor quickly viewed the child's schedule and confirmed the error the parent cited. An attempt to write a response to the parent via e-mail resulted in the e-mail bouncing back. What next?

This scenario is a typical version of many in which individuals are seeking help or an answer from the school in a time-sensitive manner, and the common refrain may be to deal with it next week. This is not always a mistake, but it too frequently builds barriers between school and community and reinforces the concept of bureaucracy that exists in our educational institutions. In this scenario, the counselor decided she would turn that view on its side. After fixing the error in the child's schedule she decided to text the parent:

> Hi Mr. B, it's [counselor]. I got your message and didn't want the weekend to go past without reaching out to you. Thanks for bringing the error to my attention. Your daughter's schedule has been updated—you should be able to see this on your end. Let me know if you have any questions and enjoy the last weekend of summer!

It should be mentioned that the parent's voicemail detailing this problem was very polite but concerned, even tense. The follow-up response was priceless.

> Wow, that was quick. My wife and I are so grateful that you took the time out of the beginning of your weekend to resolve this. I have never had someone take the time to reach out like this; what an amazing first impression! I am already all over Facebook talking about how great this is and your school is!

Think about the power of public relations here: You corrected a problem that could have—and often does—result in someone complaining, "I can't believe this! Here we go again, another blunder by the school system. It's no wonder everyone can't stand the system. Could you imagine if any other organization ran customer service like this!?!"

This was effectively flipped. Indeed, organizations that resolve issues quickly and communicate the correction effectively engender greater loyalty than organizations where individuals have never encountered a problem! It is in the attack of the problem and prompt follow-up, rather than seeking perfection, that gains are made and positive relationships fostered. We are all human, and most people recognize human error. It is the disregard for this that angers those looking for help.

I WANT AN IMMEDIATE INVESTIGATION AND ACTION!

Because we are human, emotions get the best of adults involved with schools. Sometimes and this seems to perpetuate with children, who parents, teachers and community members feel so strongly about. [AU: I'm not sure what you are saying here—I think some words may be missing? please clarify.] We model appropriate behavior for children. Because of human nature, adults also make mistakes and feel pressured to demand action.

At times we feel the assault coming at us, be it from a parent, a colleague, or even a boss. It is at these moments when we are most vulnerable and feel most pressured. A defensive posture brings our primal instincts out, and that is bad news in modern-day interactions. A demand sounds so strong, forceful, and convincing that we feel compelled to act. This is a mistake. It is exactly at this moment when we must take a step back, employ a measured response, and be the rational adult in the exchange. After all, there needs to be at least one adult managing the hostile exchange, and it's a good bet you can't count on the other person.

There is a simple and effective microstrategy that helps protect you and at the same time helps the other person to step back long enough to tap out of his or her animal instincts and restart. The example here is based on a scenario of an investigation demand, but this can work under any circumstance when you are being challenged, pressured, and rushed to respond. It helps you regain control and puts you in a strong position.

Here it is: "I am sorry about your concern. We will address it without rushing to judgment, according to the district/school/my procedures, and once a determination is made we will provide a response proportionate to the matter." This statement has far-reaching results that may not appear obvious, yet they are there, in time-tested battle scenes, over and over again.

Let's break this statement down to provide the rationale for its effectiveness as a microstrategy. First, we are not dismissing the concern, so the individual cannot use this as a point of contention to go above our heads or cause harm to efforts to help children. Second, and most important, you are setting the tone that you will not be fazed by the individual's pressure or demand. You will respond as appropriate to the findings and thoroughly investigate, which buys you time. Granted, this may indeed be a substantial response, but often it is not. That's because many demands placed on us as educators are the result of misinformation the person is either receiving or interpreting. Once a response is made, you are compelled to respond in an evenhanded manner, regardless of the accusation.

THE ID POLICE: PUT PRIDE ASIDE AND INSTEAD ELIMINATE THE PROBLEM

In most schools today, students are expected to wear IDs as part of ever-increasing security measures. Most kids comply. For a variety of reasons, some persistently refuse to comply, and adults are found battling with these children. In one school, there was a child we'll call Seth, who never arrived at school in the morning with his ID.

The school was vigilant about requiring that students wear their ID, and swiftly sent students for a replacement daily to reinforce the expectation. Students needing replacements were fined, and in Seth's case the bill was adding up. For the 2 percent of children who, like Seth, repeatedly come unprepared, this turns into an opportunity to avoid class, something a child with other challenges may in fact seek as an avoidance tactic. By its very attempt to reinforce its expectations, the school was losing Seth.

The purpose of wearing an ID in schools is to strengthen security measures, and this makes logical sense. Like hospitals that require doctors to wear badges that allow them unique access to sensitive areas or banks that require employees to wear them while managing money, schools must maintain a level of security to ensure the safety of students and adults. Yet cornering a child and adding fines to a family that will likely never be able to afford to pay is, frankly, absurd.

We may feel compelled to require students to wear an ID or follow some other standard or expectation, but in Seth's case, and in the cases of so many children like him, he simply did not have the structures in place in his home life to come to school regularly prepared with his ID. It's that simple. If the purpose is to have the child wear an ID and the current system is not working, why bother continuing?

Why not consider an alternative, practical solution and eliminate the problem? It is a common aphorism that "the definition of insanity is doing the same thing over and over again but expecting different results." Let's consider this from a practicality standpoint. Once an orderly system, falling in line with dress code, now fades with relevance. Therefore, consider asking, what's worth fighting for and at what cost?

A workshop presenter once shared the intriguing story of the rise and fall of the Remington typewriter. Remington went through a series of milestones, forever bettering its product, until one day the company created its fastest, most accurate, easiest to use, and most reliable typewriter. It was the typewriter of all typewriters. It was simply genius. It was unfortunately also already obsolete by the time Remington went into production with it. The late twentieth century brought with it a technology revolution. Computers and the internet made the best-ever Remington typewriter unnecessary.

Some of our best ideas can seem ingenious and yet, at the same time, sadly out of touch, better suited to a bygone era. Anyone who has grown up professionally in a school community that values education can recall a time when forcing compliance on children was quite simply a part of institutionalizing the process expected and produced the outcome of a civilized, well-performing classroom. Yet was it really easier?

> The children now love luxury; they have bad manners, contempt for authority; they show disrespect for elders and love chatter in place of exercise. Children are now tyrants, not the servants of their households. They no longer rise when elders enter the room.

Though some of the language in the quote by this educator might hint at a different era, the context certainly sounds familiar to the oft-quoted contemporary teacher challenges, looking with nostalgia at a time when there was greater compliance, possibly shrouded in the appearance of respect. This quote, in fact, is from one of the great educators of all time, none other than the philosopher Socrates, in roughly 400 BCE. Sometimes we need to be reminded of perspective before a problem can truly be seen practically to allow us to eliminate issues that persist.

Teachers have hard jobs. They are expected to meet high demands while managing the potential chaos of student misbehavior. It is important to frame this in the context that we must hold students accountable to a school community's values. At the same time, adapt to recognize the resolution to students not wearing IDs that teachers seek. We must consider a simple and effective microstrategy to resolve this dilemma. We do this by putting our pride aside, and changing our *approach*, not our *expectations*. There is no script to use with difficult children and children in difficult circumstances.

If teachers can embrace the tools offered here—even if these tools seem to fly in the face of conventional wisdom—these teachers will be empowered by having access to these ideas to be change agents to solve a problem. Armed with a flexible approach and willingness to attack the problem from a different angle, teachers can discover that saying, "It won't work" only creates a self-fulfilling prophecy. Let's look at an elimination of the problem rather than this ineffective approach that fosters broader implications.

Returning to the ID-less Seth, the principal called him in to discuss the issue, which was written up as a referral by his homeroom teacher after repeat "offenses." Seth already had ten ID fines, and they both knew these would never be paid. Worse, each time Seth took the trip to get his ID replacement, he often lost fifteen to twenty minutes of valuable instructional time, a tremendous loss for a child already behind.

Before long, Seth was being confronted by security officers and teachers on duty questioning why he was loitering in the hall again. He now felt targeted, a typical refrain from a child in his circumstance, and the adults intervening felt disrespected when he griped. This was a self-perpetuating cycle, and the school was further losing a child who needed a different solution to this problem.

The principal discussed the issue with Seth. It was clear that when Seth left school at the end of the day, he went to a home filled with chaos. It may not even be his fault that sometimes his IDs were left out and eventually discarded or lost in some corner of his home. Remember the purpose: to have him wear his ID daily and not have to replace it every day, further eliminating hallway loitering.

The principal suggested a unique solution: When Seth arrived at his homeroom class, his teacher would hand him his ID; then, during his last class period at the end of the day, the teacher would collect the ID from him just prior to his departure. Then the last period teacher would put the ID in the homeroom teacher's mailbox on her way out each afternoon, and the ID would subsequently be picked up by the homeroom teacher the next morning. Seth was offered a solution that adults would help him with. Would it work? Perhaps the question might be, why wouldn't it work?

Since this arrangement was instituted, not a day has gone by that Seth hasn't had his ID on: in class, in the halls, at lunch. He is no longer found loitering around the building, costing himself valuable learning time. He is no longer questioned by the ID or loitering police. He is in a classroom, learning and growing. Sometimes Seth argues, takes his ID off, and must be reminded to put it back on, all in the safety of a classroom. He complies, and the problem has been eliminated.

Some would argue that this is cheating or giving Seth a leg up. So what? It's working. The lesson here is that applying a unique solution can eliminate the problem and help minimize a cascade of problems that endure beyond the original issue, something that is a typical refrain for at-risk children.

The broad scope of this simple microstrategy is that a culture of care provides a proactive method for helping a child. The example here is about an ID, yet the microstrategy can be applied in far broader contexts to eliminate issues and in simple, cost-effective ways can change school culture. Yet again, the power of persuasion overcomes the force to comply.

CHAPTER SUMMARY

1. *The $6 T-shirt.* Use small incentives to make a positive competitive environment, which motivates students to achieve your desired objective.
2. *Who Do You Sit Closer to in a Difficult Conversation between Two People?* Always sit next to the most difficult person in this scenario. This may sound intimidating, but that is exactly why we proactively defuse by using proximity control to foster more direct human interactions and rebuild relationships in hostile situations.
3. *Use Your Cell Phone.* Go against conventional wisdom by utilizing this strategy, building great PR, and knowing that if and when you need to, you can also block or ignore those who abuse the professional side of cell phone correspondence.
4. *I Want an Immediate Investigation and Action!* When confronted with aggressive, demanding, and angry parents, if you cannot get to the issue in the time expected, use this strategy to temporarily pause, build a rational response, and allow yourself to gain control over your response.
5. *The ID Police: Put Pride Aside and Instead Eliminate the Problem.* Educators can eliminate issues in more extreme circumstances by looking beyond ordinary methods of enforcement and instead fix the issue, eradicating future recurrences.

Chapter Three

The One-Liners That Disarm Any Parent, Student, or Others in Difficult Situations

Educators are under pressure to meet deadlines that are made more daunting when faced with time-consuming, energy-draining confrontations. This creates obstacles that are costly in terms of work-life balance. Using the right approach, an effective response to these inevitable challenges will significantly reduce the time required and simultaneously improve the issue. (Note my use of the word "reduce," not "eliminate.")

No one can completely restore all the lost time and energy that results when educators are distracted from their work and professional growth. Therefore, it is important to recognize that these challenges inevitably surface, and that when they do, simple, effective techniques can go a long way in reducing the time spent managing them. The right approach can also help to build long-term trust and establish relationships. Following are several time-tested techniques that tackle these intermittent occurrences and turn them around.

SILENCE

A new principal sat in his office with his assistant principal while a parent chastised him over the phone about an issue involving her child. This all-too-common story line is a regular occurrence for administrators and teachers. How do you respond to such a tongue-lashing? The mistake of fighting back is instinctive yet destructive. Understanding this—and following several fruitless attempts to interject a response, during which the parent interrupted him again and again—he turned to his assistant principal and quietly mouthed, "Watch this."

The parent continued with her belligerent tirade, not hesitating, for several minutes. Finally, she ran out of gas, with nothing more to add, audibly sounding out of breath. The principal sat quietly across from his assistant principal, with his finger to his mouth to gesture, "Don't respond." For the assistant principal, it was awkward enough to watch her boss let the tongue-lashing go on unchecked, and now he wasn't responding at all?

After what seemed like a pause of at least fifteen to twenty seconds, the parent said, "Hello?"

The principal quietly responded, "Yes?"

The parent said, "Oh, I thought I lost you."

"No," replied the principal. "I just didn't know when you were finished because I tried several times to answer your questions and address your concerns but you kept interrupting me. Are you finished?"

This response may sound audacious, even sarcastic or worse, completely blind to the parent's objectionable behavior. Yet let's look under the hood and see what happened next, and why. This strategy may seem counterintuitive, and effective microstrategies are often just that. That is why they work: The completely unexpected reaction flips the approach of a person in a difficult conversation like this one with almost instant success.

Difficult people and people in difficult situations are accustomed to fighting. And they are good at it. As educators, we strive for peace and harmony in our classrooms and schools. We are not fighters. Anytime you attempt a battle under this type of circumstance, you will lose. More important than the damage to your personal pride, you will lose in your attempt to return the issue to helping the child. This is what matters more than winning the argument, pride, or a moment of satisfaction such as hanging up on a parent (which has its own repercussions!).

Always remember that no matter how irrational, emotionally charged, or objectionable a person is on the other end of the line, it is never about you. More importantly, remember that there is a child caught in the middle of this battle. The way to stop the conflict and bring the real objective to the surface is to do the unexpected. Silence is surprising to belligerent people. They are accustomed to a response, albeit often a helpless one given their expertise at arguing. Yet they still need something from you: help with their child. That is your power.

When a hostile parent, child, colleague, or other person awaits your combative response, ready to pounce, and instead they receive silence, the awkward pause provides crucial time to reinforce in their brain what just happened, what they just did. The response reinforces a chance to acknowledge their actions, a way to pause and reflect before going on an attack again.

When attack is met with silence, the attacker does not have an equal partner in aggression.

The principal has used this tactic hundreds of times since and has yet to come across any angry person who didn't respond with some variation on, "Oh, okay. I'm sorry, I'm just really upset about this and no one has done anything about it." A door has opened, one that allows the principal to liberate parents from a sense of helplessness, which, as difficult as it may be to see, is in fact what they are feeling.

Acknowledging that the person is upset provides a window of opportunity to seize upon. The simplicity of the real objective makes it feasible and actionable, and redirects a parent without ever scolding or pitting for a fight. This is a win-win for the child caught in the middle. Try this in your next interaction and see the outcome enabling you to get to resolution without making enemies out of the agitated person on the other end of the line.

AGREE RATHER THAN RESPOND

A middle school was working to engage nonteaching staff in positive intervention with their student body. This model was oriented toward a positive behavior support in schools approach. The intent was to convey to the nonteaching faculty that they were empowered to control their zone with an intervention approach rather than punishments that often created hostile interactions, rendering them powerless in working with children.

The assistant principal met with bus drivers, aides, and cafeteria staff as part of this process. She worked diligently to craft the perfect slideshow and inspire the staff for a new school year with better-behaved students. As she surveyed the group, several highly agreeable looking individuals smiled, affirmatively and excitedly agreed with a positive approach, an incentive-based program to motivate children in their charge.

Yet in the back of the room sat a bus driver, leaning back and appearing disinterested with a sour look on her face. Her presence was intimidating, but the assistant principal kept going. After several of the highly agreeable individuals got up and collected lottery tickets that they were encouraged give out to their students when children exhibited good conduct. These tickets are issued to serve as a motivator to offer well-behaved students.

It is often moments like these that define you can tip the balance of acceptance, influenced by such an intimidating presence and informal power as this driver. Her intimidation has the potential to alter the course of perception and effectively shoot down all hope for getting the previously well-intentioned and especially the fence-sitters on board. (Fence-sitters are those who are almost in but need some encouragement and direction; they are the members of your staff who tip the balance in one direction or another.) Our response, in one simple reaction, can have a cascading effect on this entire group, and this impacts everything from school culture to discipline numbers in the school. It is a powerful, often missed impact.

The assistant principal had observed one too many interactions between combative staff and administrators that caused a goal to self-destruct simply because of the wrong reaction by leadership. These reactions include panic, losing focus, and, worse, making it about compliance. In all these instances, the leadership lost the fence-sitters and the whole framework of the idea fell like a house of cards. It doesn't have to be that way.

Having observed the destruction that one challenging statement can make—how the wind in the sails of an idea can impact a hope, a goal, a vision, a dream—we should never argue with this view. In fact, we should embrace it. Do this with students in classes, teachers in faculty meetings, or, as in the scenario described here, with a bus driver in a meeting to reduce discipline. The assistant principal's response echoed far beyond that room filled with a group of hard-working blue-collar workers. It echoed through the halls and into the community.

"You're right, it is so elementary. That's the beauty of it: This system is so simple, anyone can do it!"

There was a pause, and a moment later, big smiles spread across the audience. The assistant principal thinks she even saw her doubter move her mouth from a sourpuss to a neutral position. A process for engaging non-teaching faculty in a school-wide positive behavior support system began. It has successfully remained in place at this school for years, and it happened because of a very simple, noncombative, and effective tactic: Agree rather than respond.

It is human nature to become defensive when our ideas are challenged—especially about kids and what we are passionate about. Fresh off a training on positive behavior support in schools, the assistant principal was excited about reducing discipline, improving school culture, helping students, enhancing relations with parents and more. A wrong turn in her response could have taken all that down, as it so often does when dealing with informally powerful people. Setting pride aside allows us to seize on, and even capitalize on, a moment. When challenged about an idea, don't disagree with it; instead, use the person's own words to transform fence-sitters into believers.

WHY SHOULD WE BE ANY DIFFERENT?

One day early in December an outstanding seventh-grade science teacher walked into the principal's office, steaming mad. She had just had it out with a boy who was the most difficult child ever. He had a typical "most difficult child in the school" story: His mother had left his father, his twin brother, and him several years ago. His father was paralyzed from a work accident that happened a few years ago and he had a substance abuse problem, the natural progression of a problem resulting from the pain he endured and the drugs to help—another tragic victim of the opioid crisis. And so the boy—we'll call him Ryder—and his brother were left for the school to raise.

The teacher began explaining in the heat of her frustration, "I want him out of my class. He is disrespectful; he is disruptive to the other students. I have never, in all my years as a teacher, had to deal with such a bad, disrespectful child! And there are enough other bad kids in that class, let alone him. I can't teach with him in there; I need him moved out of that class!" Some administrators may respond to a teacher with her respect level by collapsing. Others may push back. Neither scenario nets a good outcome for the teacher, the class, or, worst of all, the child.

The assistant principal leaned back in his chair, listening intently, letting her unload. And then he said something, expressionless, that was very surprising to her: "Okay, I'll move him tomorrow."

She looked at him with surprise and simply asked, "What?" He repeated this statement, and she responded, "Oh, okay . . . so that's it?"

"Yes," he replied, "that's it."

She slowly got up and edged out of the room, saying, "Okay, well, I guess . . . I will put the form in to change him, right?"

"Right." Then he said to her, "Oh, Tina, just one more thing: I want you to consider that he is used to being let down by adults. He expects you to give up on him, just like every other adult has in his life, so why should we be any different? I just want you to be aware of that when you look at his empty seat in class every day, when you see him walking aimlessly in the halls and are tempted to think, 'What a relief!'"

Tina slumped back down in the chair and said, "Okay, I get it! But how do you deal with a kid like this?"

He replied, "You do the exact opposite thing to what everyone else has done that hasn't worked. You stop yelling. You keep him in at lunch. You be the one adult in his life who holds him accountable and gives him love—tough love. And you do it with your arm around him the whole time—figuratively speaking."

The principal has presented this scenario to a total of ten educators, nine of whom responded in the same way Tina did. To this day, many of those teachers share stories of children like Ryder going off to the navy or a trade school or maybe even college—and coming back to thank them. And if they remember nothing else positive about the adults in their life, they will remember that one adult who held them to the same standard and gave them the same love they gave their own children, the opposite reaction to what they were expecting. This can change kids' lives in ways that go beyond our own understanding.

This approach can work with anyone, anywhere, who charges in with a demand. Nine out of ten? Those are better odds than forcing someone to keep sending referrals to your office or just caving and farming every difficult child out. If educators could get nine-out-of-ten chances to save the riskiest children, that would be incredibly beneficial and worth the energy and resources. Keep this in mind whenever you are confronted with an agitated, albeit understandably upset, person wanting change in your school. Fortunately, those of us in schools have a human touch that, once we are signaled about what really matters in teaching children, reframes our perspective almost instantly.

I DEMAND AN IMMEDIATE CALL/MEETING!

Many times, the misinformation conveyed to others through students—or worse, social media—escalates the anger of a person who may incorrectly feel you wronged them and did so with contempt. As noted throughout this book, almost all educators are caring, dedicated individuals who got into education because they wanted to help children. It is therefore astonishing to us when this happens, especially to the very best and most dedicated teachers. It is also surprising how often it seems to come up and with such intensity.

Often, we cower in fear at the fury propelled at us and only make matters worse by not responding. Leaving a concern unanswered may be worse than answering it unsuccessfully because the angry person feels ignored. Or sometimes we are just too busy to stop what we are doing and address the concern. In either case, we need a quick and effective response that deflects this pressure long enough so we have time to get to it and at the same time keeps the other person from feeling as if he or she is being dismissed with contempt, which was never our intent in the first place.

Think about the times when you wanted or needed help with a problem and you felt ignored, brushed off, uncared for, and unattended. We have all run into this appalling kind of customer service. This may elicit feelings of a time when we were so offended we abandoned loyalty toward a business—or we were ourselves that angry and aggressive person on the other end of the phone! Remember this anytime a person lashes out at you: It is not about you, and it is coming from an aggravated state of mind, rational or not, that this person is insisting you help. What if you can't or you need to get some answers first?

Like so many of our microstrategies, one simple response technique can effectively can set things back on track, where you most need them centered. Remember, whether you fear the person's aggressiveness or don't have the time to respond to the demand for action, you can buy time to collect yourself and investigate the matter. This all starts with a simple statement: "Your concern is important to me, which is why I don't want to rush to respond in error. I want to give you, and this concern, the time you deserve and provide you an informed response."

This strategy has proven almost foolproof. Remember that I am not presenting ideas that are perfect, but rather those that are time-tested and worth using because of the likelihood that they will reduce the challenges you face and save you time. You still need to give an answer, but you've bought back critical time and lessened the likelihood that the individual will go above your head. This also helps to set the tone for future interactions.

By following up thoroughly, you are proving that you did in fact take the time to investigate and address the concern, and that you will do it again. What's more, you have shown that you are not ignoring the person and that you will follow up, which often sets the stage for a more reasonable response from the next unreasonable person in the future.

"I'M GOING TO SUE YOU!" WHEN SOMEONE PULLS THE LEGAL CARD

It is because we live in a litigious society that when more challenging individuals act, they resort to threats, often with legal action. One educator described this reality thus: "I have been threatened with being sued by someone over a hundred times" (although he has never actually been sued!).

The reality is most people who choose to use the legal card fail to recognize that education law operates under very different principles than their lawyer comprehends or their friends at a local barbecue know about. And many believe they can sue their way out of whatever issue or concern they face with a school or educators they disagree with. Even if they do know that their threat will not go anywhere, they may be using it as a vehicle to get what they want from you or the school.

Putting aside the misunderstanding that faces individuals who believe their issue can and will be addressed through legal threats, we have a true and ethical responsibility to help. Getting back to this premise not only helps, it gets individuals away from the exhaustive and counterproductive nature of combative primal instincts of threats like, "I'm going to sue you." So how do we do this? Always bring this back to the child. Always bring this back to help and support the greater interest of that child or children. This can be accomplished at the onset, when someone is insinuating legal action, or at the other end, when the person is determined to sue!

Here are two illustrations at either end: the person who is using the threat to get action and the person who is already prepared to act. The first involves a parent who wanted her twins to have the same teachers in their new school.

In her initial contact, the parent referenced the law, which requires schools to do their best to accommodate having twins in parallel or same-teacher classes:

> Per the attached NJ Law A1671, I request that Dennis and Alexa be kept in the same classroom/house. I understand that they have different electives, but I would like them to be together in the rest of their classes, if possible. If this is not possible, I would like the school to discuss this with my lawyer.

Here is the response from the school:

> Don't worry about the law, we would make this happen anyway. One recommendation I have—they have the same teachers but different classes. Almost all twins prefer this arrangement—it allows for same-teacher assignment consistency while offering some individual identity for themselves, something critical in adolescent development.

This had the effect of getting the parent away from her focus on the law and the jump she had already made to getting a lawyer involved, both now and in the long term, and to understanding that the school cares, beyond and regardless of legal requirements. This is a powerful message communicated by the school. It sets the stage for future matters and presumes that the school always wants to do the right thing not because of legal consequences, but, more importantly, because it cares.

The second illustration involves a more hostile, frustrated individual further down the road:

> I expect a guarantee, in writing, that my child won't be bullied again, or you will have to deal with my lawyer. I will sue you and the school; you will be held personally responsible. I demand you do this!

This type of legal challenge requires a direct response. The father was clearly upset that his child was being bullied and believed the school was not doing enough to stop it. Here is the school official's response:

> I'm sorry about what is happening with your child. I want to help. I cannot do that when the threat of your lawyer is presented. If you want our lawyers to discuss this, that is your right. If you want me to help, I can do that. Do you want to take legal action, or do you want me to help by working directly with you?

This educator was effective in turning the attention back to the child, reiterating the fact that the school cares, and offered two options: Have our lawyers talk, which will take longer and be less direct, or let me intervene directly. This was an effective way to redirect an angry, understandably emotional parent back to working with the school to resolve the problem in a way that was less costly for both and helped refocus the concern on the best method for intervention.

TRANSFORM ANY CONSPIRACY THEORIST INTO YOUR MOST LOYAL ALLY

New Jersey law requires that students be immunized for their eleventh birthday. This is a small window, and if schools do not comply, the state fines the district for each unimmunized student who is present without a religious exemption. One school struggled with collecting immunization documentation from families, who were understandably confused, either not recognizing the small window or not understanding the significance of the requirement that must be followed by schools and families to get immunized.

Several alerts were issued explaining the importance of meeting this requirement and that the school would have no choice but to withhold important information from the family in the absence of this documentation. In order to boost parental response to fulfill this requirement, the school nurses and principal determined it necessary to temporarily withhold student schedule access until the requirement was satisfied, at which time the child's new schedule could be released.

This certainly increased responsiveness and became a standard procedure to ensure high response rates annually. Yet one parent took issue with the process. She was offended by being forced to bargain for her daughter's schedule. She demanded her daughter's schedule and called the superintendent's office ready for a fight. What do you do when someone armed and ready to fight presents this scenario to you? Remember that we are educators. Here's how this played out.

The parent arrived at the school, insisting to see her daughter's schedule before school orientation, regardless of her lack of compliance. "This is illegal!" she exclaimed. The secretary visited the principal at his desk with a concerned and cautionary look on her face: "Mrs. Insistence is here, demanding her daughter's schedule be released to her, but she hasn't submitted her child's immunization documentation. She says her daughter is immunized and has her paperwork, but she refuses to submit it, as she described, based on receiving a trade for her schedule." The principal smiled, contemplating that he did not, in fact, have to fight this parent.

The principal went out to the front office, greeted the parent with a cheery, "Hello!" and listened to her as she delivered her demands in the same harsh tone described by the secretary: ". . . And I demand to have my daughter's schedule right now!"

The principal replied, "So you're telling me that you have the immunizations?"

"Yes!"

"No problem; here is your daughter's schedule."

The secretary watched as the principal happily handed the student's schedule over to her mother. "Thanks for being honest with me," he added.

The parent paused awkwardly, in disbelief, and said, "Oh, okay . . . ummm, thank you. I'll bring the immunizations back tomorrow."

He replied, "No problem. Bring them back whenever you can before school starts, and welcome to the middle school!"

The parent didn't bring the immunization documents back the next day, or even the following week. Rather, she brought them two hours later. There is an important lesson in why this was such effective tactic. The principal took a risk and trusted the parent. Giving trust a chance paid off. By offering unconditional trust and belief, the principal successfully elicited the response he desired from this mother. She changed her perspective in seconds, from an angry mother, possibly upset about her own memories of school rules that seemed bureaucratic and insensitive—*How dare they withhold my daughter's schedule as collateral!*

This parent was used to fighting. She fights with the cashier at Target, the phone operator, and the traffic officer making her await safe passage. She fights all day, every day. Yet that day, the script was flipped. Life became far easier for the next few years in dealing with that parent, whose loyalty was gained in ways you cannot buy with force.

You may wonder if this was a reckless move by the principal. Was he defying a district standard by offering discretion in this scenario? What if she went on social media and told her friends how you can just push this guy around? In truth, it was calculated and possibly risky—but well worth it.

The start of a parent's journey, especially a parent who may harbor distrust or distaste based on her own perceptions of school operations, is a great time to win an ally, or at least reduce the likelihood she will attack the school in the future. Maybe this parent would not have returned with the immunization documentation. This does not change the requirement and the school would have ultimately cordoned off any child who arrived without proper paperwork. Most often, that doesn't have to happen when you offer trust to a person high on the "principle of the thing." Start with trust and you will be surprised at how often and how effectively it pays off.

HOW DID YOU KNOW?

One day in October, when leaves were still falling, a young teacher saw students causing a ruckus in the hall, serious enough that it violated the school's code of conduct. He intervened and most of the students ceased and apologized—except for one. The teacher had been warned about this child: disrespectful, argumentative, and challenging.

Trained as a special educator, the teacher felt confident he could overcome the barriers built by this child, who was ready for a fight aimed at rebelling against "the system." He looked much older than the others, long hair, too much facial hair for a ninth-grader. It didn't take long. When he turned to face the teacher, he started unloading the challenges.

As a teacher today, there is always a danger that you might push a student over the edge and face something serious, especially with all the media attention focused on much more extreme retaliation like the gun violence we hear about in the news regularly. Clearly, this was a show of pride and in front of his peers, his friends. This student wasn't going to back down. In his calmest, lowest voice, the teacher directed the other students to leave, and they obliged. He attempted to move the difficult student to the office, but the student refused, now cursing at the teacher. They don't teach this in college!

The teacher went to the nearest room, picked up a phone and alerted the main office. Arriving on the scene were security and an assistant principal. They tracked down the student, who was issued a suspension, and, breathing a temporary sigh of relief, the teacher wondered to himself, *But when he returns, what next?* Sure enough, several days later, the student was back at school with conditions placed on his return. Yet the teacher had a feeling those conditions wouldn't carry weight with this tough kid. He was right. What happened next set the course for the remainder of the school year.

Several days after the student's return to school, he inevitably walked in the direction that would find him face-to-face with the teacher who had reported him. The teacher expected something to happen but didn't know just what it would be. As the moment arrived, the bitter student turned his head slightly and, under his breath but loud enough to hear, said, "Homo!" A typical teacher's reaction under these circumstances might be to turn immediately toward the disrespecting student, scold him, and drag him to the office to pile on more discipline. But that's not what happened this time.

The teacher knew that reaction would never really end the battle. This kid had a battle to fight and a score to settle. Amplifying this with an equally proportionate punishment would further perpetuate the issue. So he decided to try something different, something unexpected. He stopped in his tracks, turned to the student, and asked, "How did you know?"

This completely unexpected response simply baffled the student. He mumbled something along the lines of, "Yeah, I knew it . . . " and walked away. That was the last time this student attempted to engage the teacher. Why? Let's look at the dynamics and consider how this kind of simple, behavior-altering response can shift a cascade of agitated and harmful exchanges between student and teacher.

Tough kids have tough shells. They are ready for a fight and accustomed to it. Adults in positions of authority are a worthy prize. When someone refuses to fight and instead reacts in a startlingly unpredictable manner, this shifts the accustomed reaction from a place of comfort with a difficult child to one that is foreign territory. An adult authority figure is not supposed to react like this, yet the teacher did. Now there's nowhere to go. Not only did he not get into trouble, but, judging from the reaction, the teacher is unfazed by it.

Shifting reactions like this is extremely effective, especially with the most challenging of our students. We may not be helping the student in this instance, but that was not the intent of the teacher. The goal was to shift from an ongoing battle between teacher and student to persuading the student that his challenges were irrelevant to the teacher. That's power, and it is important with a small number of excessively challenging students to alter the trajectory of their attack on you.

CHAPTER SUMMARY

1. *Silence.* In those moments when you feel instinctively compelled to respond to a confrontational, emotional person, do the reverse. The reactions will surprise you and cause more productive outcomes, which should always be our objective.
2. *Agree Rather Than Respond.* Agreeing with the difficult person in the audience, and using that as a method to overturn a challenge to your ability to move forward with a goal, works surprisingly better than trying to argue with a person who has a whole lot more experience at arguing than you do.
3. *Why Should We Be Any Different?* Taking the time to put children first, and their behaviors second in context in perspective for how it impacts the challenged child most often gives the teacher the perspective needed to reorient his or her approach toward that child and helps to make a believer of the child who expects another adult to give up on him or her, just as every other adult in their life.
4. *I Demand an Immediate Call/Meeting!* Simply respond, "Your concern is important to me, which is why I don't want to rush to respond in error. I want to give you, and this concern, the time you deserve, and provide you an informed response."
5. *Transform Any Conspiracy Theorist into Your Most Loyal Ally.* Some may come at you with the "principle of the thing" and argue not because they necessarily wish to refuse compliance but because they disagree with the method you are using. The best way to get a person

like this on your side is to start with trust. That's the principle of the thing, and most often it works with surprising effectiveness.

6. *How Did You Know?* Often when children are disrespectful, we feel compelled to hold them accountable. Understanding why they are signaling disrespect and demonstrating an unlikely response will often show students that their best efforts to anger you are unsuccessful so they stop trying.

Chapter Four

Applying the Rule of 9s to Approach Every Challenge with Success

Schools and the educators charged with educating children are responsible for upholding the ethics outlined in education law and district policy. Therefore, there are times when acknowledgement of school and district guidelines is necessary. This often happens when the school opens at the beginning of the year and at intermittent times when the school is organizing field trips, new technology upgrades, or other initiatives. This can be as simple as having students and parents review a classroom management agreement. We are all familiar with these rules of engagement, and most individuals agree, sign off, and go about their day.

I REFUSE TO SIGN THAT!

There are always a few (typically less than 10 percent) in the school community who, for a variety of reasons, argue about various procedural mechanisms. They may contest that it's the principle of the thing, or they might fear unrealistically severe repercussions in the unlikely event such an agreement is violated. Some individuals may simply want to argue because that's what they enjoy. Regardless of the reason, there is a very simple and effective way to handle almost all these instances. Most important, this simple microstrategy aligns to whatever the agreement is, and you don't have to get caught in the crosshairs of a fight.

A teacher approached her principal one day early in the year with a startled look that said, "Help me!" She showed him a parental response to the code of conduct agreement sent annually to parents. The tone was abrupt and intimidating. It went something like this:

> I received your school's code of conduct agreement and reviewed it. I question why a school needs a signature because if there ever is an issue, I may not agree with the action taken, and will take my own legal action to defend my child with whatever resources I have at my disposal. Do not send home requests for my signature ever again. Your job is to teach my child and serve to fulfill my taxpayer dollars, not to hold me hostage to a bogus agreement.

One can imagine the distress of this teacher, eager to do what she loves—working with children to help them grow—who receives such a threatening response. Consider her dilemma: She is expected to collect these responses, which all her other students' parents returned. Will there be a consequence for her if she does not receive a response from this parent? Of course not. Yet as educators, we are characteristically rule followers, and the fear persists and it feels real. So now what?

An effective and supportive educational leader will either guide the teacher accordingly or model a response to this parent. In either case, the teacher will feel supported and subsequently learn from the principal's response. In this situation, the principal did take appropriate action, informing the teacher that she would reply and copy the teacher. Relieved, yet still somewhat nervous about this parent, the teacher read the principal's response:

> Dear Mrs. Jones,
> Thank you very much for responding to the school's code of conduct guidelines. Your child's teacher shared your response with me. I want to assure you that your signature is not necessary. By replying, you have already acknowledged receipt and review of the school's code of conduct. I hope that your child has a wonderful year here at our school. We are here to support his success. Let me know if you have any questions.

After the principal sent this reply, the teacher asked in surprise, "Can we do that?" The principal replied, "Why not?" Here was this principal's premise: We should never get caught up in the minutiae of legal battles with anyone over details that someone contests with such intensity and alarm. The school is an organization that is expected to educate children and to do so in a safe and orderly manner. As educators, we work every day to sustain this orderly and safe environment. It is our job, our expectation.

Not only did the principal acknowledge receipt to ensure the standard had been met for this child's parent, but she skillfully thanked the parent for that acknowledgement. This response would stand up in the rare instance of a legal battle, but in most instances, it will squash any battle the parent was ready for before it takes legs. Be grateful for the 90+ percent who signed off and thank the few who do not for acknowledging.

MANAGING CONFLICT OVER VALUES

American schools increasingly represent an eclectic mix of cultures, religions, races, and sexual orientations. This should always be celebrated through the lens of the rich diversity offered as the school's culture. It is an advantage most non-Americans in the world do not enjoy and offers an incredible human resource pool.

This also poses risks because diversity can result in difficulty with narrow-minded or culture-contrasted values of people accepting the one inevitable: change. Most of those who arrive at our schoolhouse doors are open-minded and value our flexibility. There are those, however, who do not. This is not a problem if it does not impede the rights of others. But what happens when it does? Let's explore one such scenario and how the school responded.

School counselors were approached by students about participating in the National Day of Silence, a day when students across the country take a solemn stand against the bullying and harassment faced by lesbian, gay, bisexual, transgender, and queer (LGBTQ) youth. The Day of Silence is a student-led national event in which participants take a vow of silence to highlight the silencing and erasure of LGBTQ people at school. To understand the challenge confronted by the event organizers and school officials, one must first understand the legal right students have to participate in such an event.

The rights of students in schools across the United States, and in Western nations in general, have been tested through case law over the decades, and peaceful protests by students are no exception. Peaceful protests are generally allowed if they do not disrupt the orderly operation of the school. Of course, there is wide latitude in interpretation of what constitutes a disruption to orderly operation, and if a school or district truly wanted to make it difficult for such an event to be organized, it could do so. However, most school officials recognize that community values should be reflected in the school community and so they understand that it is bad business to prevent a peaceful student protest.

With the foundation laid that schools will generally condone peaceful protests that do not disrupt the orderly operations of the school, there are some exceptions that can be dependent upon community or a segment of the community protests an event like the Day of Silence to be permitted. This was the case at a school in the Northeast in which the religious values of a small group conflicted with this event. A member of this community reached out to the school about their objection to the event, under the auspices that the individual's child was negatively impacted by being exposed to this.

Remember that this event was student organized and facilitated. The school did not coordinate the event; it simply permitted students to organize and participate, and school officials informed the community. The school is on firm legal footing to support students planning and executing this event.

The delicate balance between knowing one has sound legal footing and respecting the cultural values of a small group in the community matters absolutely. If the school is pressured to deny students the right to demonstrate, the likelihood of bad social media exposure, never mind refusing students their legal right prevents schools from choosing to prohibit. Ignoring the parent's objections may not seem nearly as significant, yet the concern remains. Therefore, this is more a concern of a moral response to the parent, rather than a legal one. Being tuned in to the reality that moral concerns can carry the same weight as legal concerns is wise, and school officials should remain vigilantly sensitive in their response.

A proactive response in anticipation of such an objection allows the school to stand on firm moral ground from the explanation provided to parents, who are often surprised that students—whom they view as minors who need protections and who carry no rights—indeed possess a right to protest.

This is especially the case with community members who hold strong, deep-seated religious and cultural values that allow no one except adult males such rights to express themselves. Even they have limitations. A good idea here, then, is to reference legal case studies or valid online discussions that support and explain in layman's terms why this right exists and how the school is bound to respond.

One school found a helpful resource (Lambda Legal, 2019) that provides the firm legal footing and explains in a concise yet professional manner that the school does not support or condone the legal protest. Rather, the school remains neutral; like law enforcement maintaining order at a publicly organized protest, the school must do the same. Therefore, the school would not allow protesters to put the children whose family values contrast with those of the protesting students in a place where their rights are violated. The school should be transparent and vocal about this. The more obvious this balance of respect is, the better the day of the organized event and school day will go.

Here is an example of a communication a school might send out to the school community about its basis for allowing students to organize a Day of Silence event:

> Dear Parents,
> On April 12, 2019, some students will be participating in the nationally recognized Day of Silence. While we recognize that there may be strong feelings on either side of this issue, it is important for parents and staff to be aware that students have rights to organize peacefully. For more information, I thought it would be helpful to reference two areas that pertain to student rights: Do students have the right to participate in, and advocate for, the Day of Silence (or not to participate)?

In most circumstances, yes. Schools must respect students' right to free speech. The right to speak includes the right not to speak, as well as the right to wear buttons or T-shirts expressing support for a cause as long as this support does not disrupt the learning process. This does not mean students can say—or not say— anything they want to at all times.

There are some limits on free speech rights at school. Students cannot disrupt the orderly operations of schools during instruction. School officials are not allowed to discriminate against students based on their message. In other words, school officials may not censor a student just because they disapprove of the student's ideas, because the student's speech makes them uncomfortable, or because they want to avoid controversy. Schools cannot censor students unless they use lewd or foul language, promote illegal drug use, harass other students, or substantially disrupt the school environment.

Can a school restrict student speech because it offends other students or parents? No. So long as student expression is not lewd or profane, does not advocate violence or illegal activity, and does not harass others, schools cannot restrict student speech simply because some students or parents find it offensive. We cannot prohibit the expression of an idea simply because others find the idea itself offensive or disagreeable.

It is important to note that as school officials we recognize students' rights to peacefully not speak on this day, and we also respect the rights of students who peacefully disagree. ("National Day of Silence: The Freedom to Speak [Or Not]," 2019)

As outlined in this correspondence, the school has communicated what can and cannot be done to control the protest. This can effectively shift the blame—and the individual's value concerns—away from the school, which is adhering to the law. A school can foster the environment necessary while balancing the values of others.

Because the school should never take sides, it is important to balance this with what is conveyed to students participating. Here is what the school communicated to students protesting:

Just as you have a right to protest by not speaking, others have a right not to, and as a democratic principle, there should be no pressure placed on any student from either perspective.

I REFUSE TO LEAVE UNTIL HE SPEAKS TO ME!

More than 90 percent of individuals coming to visit the main office of a school are polite, patient, and just looking for help. This is true whether it is the teacher looking for supplies or seeking the answer to a question, or the parent arriving for a meeting with someone from the school. A child taking exception with a rule or treatment by a teacher can also occupy the office's time. Whoever the individual stopping by the office is, secretaries and administrators have a flurry of visitors, all day, every day. Thankfully, the majority are understanding, and the office can support their needs before sending them on their way.

There are exceptions, however. In less than 10 percent of the cases—but what feels like so much more—a visitor is hostile, is an energy vampire, is disrespectful, or uses intimidation tactics. This is a power play to get what is wanted, whether it is as simple as attention or something more complicated. The individual is, in his or her mind, trying to gain an upper hand.

Unfortunately, busy office staff too often get caught up in the negative interaction that costs important human resource time—time indeed better spent supporting students and staff. There is a microstrategy to counter most of these instances. Let's consider one common scenario and how it was effectively addressed, as modeled by the assistant principal.

A visiting parent was demonstrating hostile body language and tone to the office staff. The secretary nervously reported this to the administrator, who was busy typing away on his computer: "A parent is here, and he seems to have a real attitude. I tried to explain that you were busy, but he's standing at the counter, expecting you to come out. He won't leave, insisting he see you now." The assistant principal pondered the situation for a moment. He had never met this parent but could tell from his secretary's reaction that he would not take no for an answer.

The assistant principal stopped typing, rose from his desk, and followed the secretary out to the front office. Instead of stopping at the counter, where a physical barrier separated him from the visiting parent, he opened the door, put his hand out, and cheerfully asked, "Hey, how are you doing?" as he introduced himself. The parent, who seemed unprepared for this level of direct interaction, took a half step backward and hesitatingly put his hand out, looking somewhat confused. The administrator explained that he had a deadline to submit something in the next few minutes and asked if the visitor would mind waiting just a few minutes longer.

The parent waited, as requested, and when he came back to the office the administrator thanked him for his patience. Regardless of the true urgency of this issue, this parent felt it was important to be seen. Maybe he had to be at a meeting or would be traveling for weeks and had to get an issue resolved. Maybe he was under intense pressure to meet his own deadline. Maybe he was just one of those people who want to push their weight around to get what they want.

Regardless, the issue was handled effectively because the administrator broke down the very barrier that gave him power by directly greeting him, showing not fear but instead a willingness to engage, and the moment shifted to a successful outcome. It is micromoments like these that define how an interaction will unfold.

When individuals want to gain an upper hand, they most frequently resort to what they know best. Often, visitors to the office will demonstrate urgency to the staff to get a response, or worse, they will use intimidation. The only way to stand up to a bully is to punch him right between the eyes—figuratively, of course, as education professionals have an important role to play in modeling appropriate behavior in the face of inappropriate behavior. By walking right through that door and greeting the parent warmly, the administrator tore down a significant barrier. The only option left for a person seeking resolution is to accept the chance to resolve the issue. That's a win-win.

DELIVERING GOOD NEWS

Reframing a positive reality for those who fear a negative outcome has a powerful impact on school community members. This works well with students, parents, teachers, and even administrators and board members. Presenting a perspective that allows this reframing is not only a good idea, it consistently reinforces that our view is far more important to our reality than we may recognize. Here is how this technique works, most of the time, and saves you time in the process. **[AU: how does it save time?]**

Because individuals who confront you with concerns almost always have only a part of the story, they fill in the gaps. Those gaps are typically inaccurate conceptions of the real truth. This is not intentional; rather, it is human nature to create a story line that fits our view of the situation. We do not want to be wrong, and we get into a protective zone, a primal place of defense, when we are challenged. This makes it difficult if we must respond to someone who has a concern when we have a more complete picture of the events that transpired.

Following is one scenario in which a counselor and teacher were confronted by an upset adult who felt his grandchild had been bullied. The child had come home and painted a fictional account of the events with himself as a bullied victim. The grandparent wanted blood. What unfolded illustrates an excellent way to manage such an encounter.

The reality in this scenario is that there was typical back and forth between students, as so often happens between adolescents. There was clearly a conflict. So how did the educators in this circumstance prevent this from unnecessarily escalating to administration, resulting in a formal bullying investigation? The solution was simple, yet effective: They framed the truth in a positive light. It worked. After the incident was investigated, the grandparent arrived at the school wanting answers. The counselor invited him into his office and smiled, stating, "I have good news for you. Your grandchild was not bullied. This was a typical case of conflict and we can resolve it."

Notice how this was framed as a positive to the grandparent. The incident was not minimized; rather, it was reframed, and managed to protect the family's pride. The child was not in trouble for lying or for being the aggressor. Instead, this was a manageable incident that could be resolved with support and counseling.

You may wonder if this works with everyone. It does not. But the vast majority of those receiving "good news" will respond favorably. Again, this is a strategy that works with most people, most of the time. Those are good odds, and it was the case with this grandparent for whom the incident was reframed, and with maintaining dignity for the family for the way in which it was delivered, a resolution was supported by the grandparent. Problem solved, and no escalation to a toxic, time-consuming, finger-pointing result.

Remember that even though "I have good news" works most of the time, with most people, there are times when it does not work. Sometimes, for reasons of pride or circumstance, individuals dig their heals in further. This happens with a small percentage of individuals and especially with those who struggle with the reality that their child may be lying. This is an affront to their own values and can be perceived as an attack on their ability to parent. The resulting challenge is often, "Are you calling my kid a liar?!?"

ARE YOU CALLING MY KID A LIAR?!?

Sometime or another, all educators have faced a parent who defends a child's version of an incident at all costs. There are many reasons why this type of irrationality edges into an otherwise seemingly logical mindset. Understanding these reasons and then how to confront this will help the educator manage a challenge such as this one.

Even the most sensible adults can have compromised judgment when it comes to their children. This makes sense when we consider the emotional connection that loving, caring parents make with their children. They offer unconditional love, which means that reason and sensibility can be compromised when a child is in need, real or perceived. This presents a real challenge for educators when a child has clearly done what all children do—misbehave—and must be redirected.

Here is the scenario: An educator brings to the parent's attention a child's misbehavior or academic integrity issue (for example, cheating), and the parent responds, "I spoke to my child, and she told me she did not do that, and my child has never lied to me." Let's begin with the belief the parents come to the table with: *My child has never lied to me.*

The reasons parents box themselves into this fixed perspective are varied and complex. Some are cultural, others are pride getting in the way, and some are both. In fact, it may feel like an assault on the character and values the parents have personally worked to teach the child. Educators face the all-too-common and uncomfortable experience of having to dispute this belief.

This can be a harsh truth to swallow, and it is necessary to approach with tact and sincerity.

Indeed, this is a daunting hurdle for educators to get over with a parent before they can even begin to address the core issue of misconduct behind the deceit. Yet there are two simple and powerful microstrategies to use that will overcome this almost every time.

In 2008, ABC News reported on a study about kids and lying behavior (Chang, 2008). In the study, two interesting findings were revealed. First, 98 percent of teenagers reported lying to their parents about issues as varied as friends, dating, and drugs. This means virtually every child has lied to their parents at some point. Second, the answer to the question why they lied to their parents was also revealed in this study. And the answer is quite honorable, odd as that may sound for a reason to lie: "They lied mostly because they tried to protect their parents from being worried," reported the lead researcher of the study.

Let's examine this for a moment, particularly how this rationale can help parents and caregivers save face, which is the most significant cause of their denial. Children who do not want to let their parents down may be creative. Yes, it is a lie, but there are different kinds of lies. Some are criminal, while others are ways to help parents or caregivers manage their own sensitivities. In a strange way, this is a kind and sensitive approach to disclosure, or rather, nondisclosure.

At the opening of school, a principal shares this study with parents, emphasizing that students grow up learning ways to manage conflict and other challenges in their lives. While not advocating an "honorable lie," the principal aims to present context for future interactions when some children are inevitably caught being dishonest.

Lying is considered a negative personal attribute, but presented in a softer context—one that appeals to a parent's better nature—it can be more readily accepted. When a child and his or her family is in a predicament with the school and lying has occurred, this approach offers a more amicable, face-saving way to resolve the issue and turn it into a learning experience.

So what if we still cannot get around the obstacle of a parent's refusal to acknowledge that his or her child is lying? You have notified the parent, but the child went home and denied the incident, and the parent calls back the next day saying something like, "I talked to my child, and he said it didn't happen that way." You are back to square one.

Time to implement the "call home together" microstrategy! This is a proactive technique that can be employed either before the lie begins or as a follow-up in future occurrences to prevent the same challenges from surfacing. This is especially helpful when you see a trend with a parent-and-child dynamic where a deceptive claim is made by the child and the parent takes it literally.

When you are anticipating that a child will change the story about what really happened in a classroom, hallway, or bus, call home together. The way to do this is to introduce the conversation, share with the parent that the child has something to say, and let the child report themselves. This is the most effective way because there is no debate. If a child is unwilling to speak or does not share the whole story, you can either fill in the gaps or summarize and then confirm with the child that this report of events is true. This allows you, the parent, and the child to move past any deceptive delays and get right to the heart of the issue to do what really matters, help this family.

CHAPTER SUMMARY

1. *I Refuse to Sign That!* Instead of getting caught in the crosshairs of parents or others who resist signing school documents, simply thank them for acknowledging receipt by their very refusal. That's power.
2. *Managing Conflict over Values.* When the rights of students conflict with the values of a group in your school, be vigilant in understanding the law and how it protects students. Do not get into subjective opinion discussions with individuals; rather, keep the correspondence objective, be proactive and transparent before the event or protest, and know that the law is on your side.
3. *I Refuse to Leave until He Speaks to Me!* In the face of belligerent behavior, we can professionally show how confident and not intimidated, but it also models behavior for those that need to see you acting professionally and warmly. Yet stand your ground and use your influential manner to set a tone that makes it sensible for the other person to follow. By doing this, you effectively gain power back by setting the standard and sticking to it.
4. *Delivering Good News.* Shining a positive light perceived negative by another person's expectation helps them shift their view. This happens whether a person is seeking justice for an incident or just demanding your attention—and they are wrong—this is a clever and productive way to correct them. This prevents a battle, does not attack their pride, and gets the truth across in an appropriate and successful way, most of the time, with most people.
5. *Are You Calling My Kid a Liar?!?* Sharing with parents that 98 percent of kids lie and that the most common reason is that they do not want to let their parents down is a way to help parents get past the challenges often encountered in these scenarios. For the rest, orchestrate phone calls home where the child can tell the parent what happened, eliminating the after-school story fabrication that often causes additional delays in getting to the root of the problem.

Chapter Five

Taking on Test Anxiety with Three Simple, Effective Strategies

Number 2 pencils and bubble sheets have been replaced by Chromebooks and online assessments, yet the fear and anxiety caused by testing remains high. In fact, there is strong evidence that anxiety in general has increased, and that because educational institutions and politicians continue to place such strong emphasis on test results as a measuring stick for everything from individual student performance to school, state, national, and global accountability, the stakes are stressing kids out.

We can debate the merits of standardized testing and the progress monitoring practices applied to measure student performance, but regardless of the debates, measuring student performance—both in standardized form and in local, formative-based measurements—is here to stay.

One way to get away from this debate and focus more practically on how to help children succeed is to consider that regardless of political positioning, students will be tested, especially to be credentialed for professional accountability. How many of us would be satisfied if the doctor performing our surgery was excused from being assessed on his or her performance as the result of opting out? Or how about the pilot who claimed the need to skip his or her flight test? It is important to keep in focus that children gain when they learn how to take on standardized assessments.

Yet as importantly is there state of well-being when they deal with a test. If a child is overanxious, or too nervous, there can be an adverse effect on their welfare, and performance likely drops. If students are capable, it would be unfortunate and detrimental to their long-term success to underperform on an assessment. Preparing them to counter this underperformance and develop a stronger more balanced mindset is not only a good idea, it should be considered essential to help them achieve.

Therefore, we can agree that testing has important and real consequences for students' likelihood of a successful trajectory through their schooling and training in professional skills. These are measuring sticks that cannot, or at least should not, be questioned. Importantly, preparing to take assessments may be viewed as a lifelong skill, since there will be many occasions where mastery is measured.

So how do we best help children manage the stressors associated with this reality? Following are several tested methods that enable students to embrace this challenge for the good of their academic and mental well-being as well as the broader standards of measurement for school systems.

WHEN YOU MOVE THE BODY, YOU MOVE THE MIND

Think about how often you take a walk, ride your bike, or go to the gym and an idea pops into your head. There is a tremendous body of research that attests to the movement of body as a stimulant for the mind (Bergland, 2014; Jensen, 2005; Pillay, 2016). The irony is that students sit for extended periods of time, especially during testing sessions, yet we expect them to be in prime focus mode. This is most challenging for students with higher energy and focusing issues; think about students who are more susceptible to attention lapses.

Innovative teachers are recognizing the benefits of right-sized seating and allow students to sit, stand, or even spread out on beanbag chairs or the floor. Yet this setup is rarely acceptable in standardized testing structures. That may change, but for now we do our students a disservice at the same time as we aid their day-to-day instructional learning when we change the rules of the game during standardized testing.

There are ways to work around the present challenges of institutional seating restrictions for standardized testing that restrict movement during assessments. For instance, you can set up movement exercises before testing each day and at intermittent scheduled breaks. Given that students sit for most of their school day, this is effective even during a nontesting day.

Remember that on testing day, students may sit for up to two hours straight. Intermittent body movement is critical to good circulation and flow, and with that, the mind flows better. A quick warm-up is effective before a test and during breaks between sections. Teachers would be wise to allocate time for this, whether it happens during standardized testing or during local assessments.

Recognizing the limitations of physical space within classrooms, there are several ways to conduct movement exercises with this space limit, even with desks, condensed together with students of twenty-five to thirty students. Have students follow an exercise routine in the classroom that fits within the confines of space. One example can be seen at http://y2u.be/O5ChXC-rHLE. Better yet, have your physical education teacher make a video. Students likely connect better with their own teachers, and engaging students with the motivation of a teacher they know is a powerful way to entice otherwise lethargic children. Additionally, you can play current energetic or motivational background music. Getting the body activated in this way is important, especially right before a long period of sitting. This kind of movement will activate children's minds to think more creatively and critically, right when they need it most.

TEST SITE VISITATION DAY

A great way to help students and faculty reduce anxiety is by scheduling a test site visitation day shortly before standardized testing week begins. This site may or may not differ from the typical classroom setting they are accustomed to.

Helping your school community get accustomed to their testing environment in a routinized way matters regardless because simulating the environment replicates the environment, both aesthetically and visually, that students would be experiencing during testing. On visitation day, the teacher proctor is situated and students get an accurate view of their testing environment. This is a concrete method for enabling students and faculty to visualize the testing environment.

Another advantage to test site visitation day is that some students do not benefit from being in the same room as other students, who cause them to be distracted or, worse, emotionally off. Discovering the dynamics of seating arrangements on a test site visitation day, where stakes are low allows for time to make the adjustment.

This is a whole lot better than waiting until the actual testing day to discover that some students just don't belong together when we are aiming to maximize their production and maintain their wellness. Additionally, errors—such as when a student who belongs in a small group is misplaced in a large group—or special accommodations that warrant an adjustment can be corrected on this day.

With familiarity comes comfort. Just being in a test site location matters, as being in that context helps students put their minds at ease. Do an announcement like the one at http://y2u.be/oNinErnXIwQ explaining that as students visit, they will realize their anticipation and anxiety are unnecessary, because they will be comforted by discovering that this new testing setting is no different a setting than a regular classroom and that they will likely know some kids. Students also get to meet the proctor. Having a test site visitation day may sound like a costly idea in terms of time, yet it is short, often lasting just the length of a typical homeroom period, and has been well received by faculty and students who have walked through the experience.

While the tone is set that the upcoming test is important, practicing the experience and seeing commonalities allows students' brains to settle into the routine in advance. Another advantage to a test site visitation day is the benefit to parents knowing about it, if parents are considering opting their child out of the assessment based on concern over their child experiencing anxiety, and hearing their child express comfort, even excitement over the test site visitation reinforces a child's comfort. If properly presented, a school can effectively build a road map for parents to better visualize this experience through communicating in a school-wide blast, and students can do what they best: tell their parents it was no big deal.

Getting parents involved in knowing about this experience, even sharing the video announcement, helps establish a positive tone around testing. Parents then can be your greatest allies in reinforcing at home the importance yet balance of mind that students gain from approaching the test with a positive mindset.

FREEWRITE TEST ANXIETIES AND DISCUSSION

There is research that demonstrates that anxiety is reduced when students write about their test worries (Harms, 2011). There are many ways to do this. One is as simple as incorporating it right into the test site visitation day described earlier. The way to do this is simple: When students are in the room with their peers and proctor, they can take a few moments to freewrite. However, this can also operate as a stand-alone method, especially during preparation for formative assessments and those that are designed to be local assessments.

Whether freewriting in anticipation of test anxiety for a standardized assessment or for a local assessment, the process can be managed through a simple exercise. Simply responding to a prompt about what their concerns are can release some anxious thoughts. Next, allow students to talk about their concerns with a partner or in a group. Finally, allow for a brief class-wide discussion about a few of the main worries. Often students say out loud, or may think privately, "Wow, others have the same worries as me. I'm not alone." That shared experience helps validate students' concerns and can be a calming experience. There is power in knowing that they are experiencing the same challenges as their peers. Students feel less isolated in their concerns and more able to embrace the challenge.

THREE-MINUTE MEDITATIONS

Mindfulness techniques and tips are everywhere, and for good reason. In the busy day of a student—or an adult—it is so important to slow down, quiet the mind, and practice simple strategies that help reduce test anxiety and offer lifelong skills for tackling worries.

Distractions are everywhere for modern students. Cell phones offer a wondrous world of endless possibilities. They also offer an infinite supply of distractions, and social media that students can access on their phones is known to increase their anxiety. This is not a small problem. Yet there are ways to harness the quiet in students' minds. The most significant of these is through slowing everything down using techniques that help students manage their minds.

Consider new methods for quick slow-down strategies. Chair yoga is an option that enables students to get in touch with their mind-body connection. A child's focus can be enhanced quickly, at the very moment we instill structures to help slow a child's mind down and therefore, the world around them. The video at http://y2u.be/SEfs5TJZ6Nk can be shown along with the exercise video discussed previously, or you can alternate these so the strategies do not become redundant. Better yet, ask a teacher trained in yoga to create a mindful breathing video.

OFFER A TEST-TAKING TIP OF THE DAY

A great way to show support as a school community using a wider approach is to have teachers and willing students discuss a strategy each day the week before and during testing to reinforce practical, simple solutions to performing better on the test, either during morning announcements, in homeroom, or at the end of the day prior to testing. Share logical tips, like making sure they arrive at school on time.

When students hear faculty or peer leaders do this, they make a stronger connection, since they usually have one or more of these teachers or are familiar with their peers. In addition to sharing within the school, blast videos out to parents the day before testing so they can reinforce this at home. An example of these short tip videos can be found at https://www.youtube.com/watch?v=TlUm6O5CeA4.

Again, all these microstrategies can operate as stand-alones or several can be combined to help reduce anxiety in advance of a major test or standardized assessment. Consider the benefits of a stacked approach: By combining several or all these microstrategies, you are compounding your efforts and increasing the likelihood that students will maximize their performance.

Any combination strengthens the benefit students receive. You may also wish to combine these with mindfulness methods or other initiatives that are locally motivated within your school community. The important and empowering opportunity to remember is that we can and should be using multiple methods to help students reduce their test anxiety.

Remember that by instilling test-taking practices in students alongside the perspective of a growth mindset, we are not only reducing their test anxiety, we are also teaching them (and ourselves) the importance of utilizing these microstrategies for life. Strategies to reduce test anxiety can indeed be generalized and applied to broader experiences of anxiety in our lives.

When we set up a framework that allows students to draw on multiple approaches, they benefit from the probability that they are better equipped to face both the assessment and their anxiety. What better way to teach than to offer short-term strategies that work as lifelong practices?

A final note on anxiety: Given the increased recognition that anxiety is a very real and rising problem for students and faculty in our schools, it is wise to offer day-to-day practices and resources in your school community. For instance, many schools offer a wellness room for students and adults. These might look different for students than they do for faculty—and they should. For instance, children often benefit from tactile strategies, such as squeeze balls and active engagement in a task that helps then shift their focus. Adults may benefit from a comfortable chair, soft music, and even aromatherapy. Offering a place of comfort that individuals can visit is both sensible and likely to improve the wellness of all those in need within your school community.

CHAPTER SUMMARY

1. *When You Move the Body, You Move the Mind.* Research supports the idea that exercising physically benefits the mind as well. Use strategies to move the body so that you also stimulate the mind, especially before a major assessment that has considerable impact on a student's success.
2. *Test Site Visitation Day.* Taking students to their real-life testing site in advance and simulating the experience is a great way to get kids to visualize the experience and reduce their anxiety.
3. *Freewrite Test Anxieties and Discussion.* Journal writing is known to help individuals put their thoughts, fears, and dreams on paper, and to make those more well verbalized [AU: **Please clarify what you mean by this.**]. Having students freewrite about their testing concerns and then talking them out together increases students' comfort about the assessment.

4. *Three-Minute Meditations.* Short-term moments meditating help students slow their minds down and gain focus. Implementing simple, practical approaches to meditation are well worth the short bursts of time taken to implement them.
5. *Offer a Test-Taking Tip of the Day.* Have teachers and willing students discuss a strategy each day the week before and during testing to reinforce practical, simple solutions to performing better on the test, such as eating a healthy breakfast and getting a good night's sleep or turning off electronics a minimum of one hour before going to bed.

Chapter Six

The Smartest Educators Steal

HANDS UP!

A new teacher, Tom, sat at his desk with his head in his hands. He had been teaching the school computer course and was struggling to gain the class's attention when they were immersed in their computers. No matter what he tried, it was virtually impossible to turn their attention away from their screens, and worse, even those who appeared to be listening did not hear his important instruction of the moment.

Then one day, he walked into the room of a veteran teacher, a master teacher who knew far less about computer technology then he did. He exited a few minutes later shaking his head in awe, spellbound by her ability to gain her students' immediate attention when it was necessary to give direction or share information. In fact, the technique she used to turn their attention away from the hypnotic computer screens was so simple, so practical, and so efficient that he wondered why he hadn't thought of it before. He asked her if he could use the method and she laughed, saying, "Sure, I don't have a copyright on it!"

This was a curious perspective, he thought, wondering why she would want to share her ideas so willingly with a new, inexperienced teacher. After all, weren't these some of her best ideas that sustained her in a different league as a master teacher? Why would she give away her best trade secrets so easily? It seemed odd to this young teacher, early in his career and unfamiliar with what truly separates the greats in the profession from the rest. It was a valuable lesson that he did not know everything about teaching and that it was fine to apply others' good ideas. This lesson in swallowing pride was one of the most instrumental in a career that would eventually flourish under this new perspective.

The technique the spellbound Tom watched the master teacher execute with such ease that day—still in the late fall of his first school year, when green grass gave way to frost just before the winter snow began—seemed elementary. How could it be so simple? All the master teacher commanded of her class was: "Monitors off; hands up!" He watched as twenty-seven students closed their laptops or turned off their computer monitors and then saw their hands shoot up above their heads.

All of them—even that child who was always last to respond, and when he did, responded more disruptively in his class—complied! After a brief pause, a matter of seconds, the teacher was able to convey a direction that the entire class quickly and precisely followed. The master teacher explained that she had modeled this behavior and positively reinforced it the first few times before students really got it right and bought in. She emphasized that they grasped that something important was being conveyed by their teacher.

Tom decided to try this in his classroom. He offered a full disclosure to his students: He had seen a great technique in his colleague's class, simple and effective, and he wanted to try with his students. He modeled it a couple of times, first on his own, as students laughed with interest, and then with the class following his lead.

Tom could see that they were interested in mimicking his body language, and as he reinforced it—"I like the way Sara, Jane, Josh, and Kamila were all following the instruction the first time"—it caught on. Years later there is an almost constant use of technology; as computer labs moved out of a corner room with exclusive air conditioning and into all classrooms with far more mobile access, this technique is more relevant than ever. It continues to work, and all because Tom, desperate for an answer early in his career, decided to steal the idea from one of his master colleagues.

DRESS CODE DILEMMAS: HOW ONE SMALL CHILD CAN CHANGE A SCHOOL

When you consider the concept of "stealing" as an educational practice, look at it from the lens of a beginner's mind. Sometimes, we are so hardened to the way that things *should* be, that we lose the real purpose or point of values and how they *can* be.

Dress code issues have existed in schools for decades, and they will continue to if children want to find their own identify. Identification through dress is a rite of passage, and the moral clashes with adults a couple of generations older than the students creates a gap in values. Yet a school had a remarkable response to one such clash, one that brought a community, the school, and, most importantly, the students together. But as fascinating as it was, the idea was not even original—it was stolen.

Children everywhere groan when they challenge the status quo and hear, "This is the way things are" without any examination of *why* things are the way they are. One day early in spring, as the first flowers warned of warming air, officials in one school were bent on making their expectations explicit and reposted the school's dress code. This would be the year the school enforced the dress code, making it clear and ensuring it was followed! But rather than the usual murmurs and griping about fairness, something intriguing happened.

A student unknown to most faculty other than her timid flash of a smile in the hall stood before the board of education at a publicly televised meeting and advocated for a more equitable dress code in the school. She came prepared, armed with a petition signed by hundreds of students. Understanding the natural reaction to become defensive, even reactive, the principal instead decided to revisit the school's dress code. Upon investigation, one thing become clear: The student was right. The dress code was neither gender neutral nor equitable.

School leadership explored current media coverage of the #MeToo movement and other groups standing up for gender equity. It was an eye-opening recognition about movements among pioneering school districts happening in locally, and across the country.

The change movement in one school district that had the most significant impact on the principal was the adoption of a neutral dress code and how this addressed gender inequality (McCombs, 2017). In this case, female students appealed in a well-prepared and passionate declaration to their board of education. The board of education and superintendent subsequently worked with the school community to revise the dress code and—just as importantly—to educate staff, parents, and students about it.

The student's presentation, which was televised, is worth a watch ("Oregon Student Dress Codes," 2016; https://www.youtube.com/watch?v=r7G7KXDI4vI). Phrases such as, "I am not a distraction" became catchphrases. The educators at the school in Oregon realized it was only a matter of time before this moved beyond the "it's not fair" argument to one of substance and heart. It was time to act.

Upon examination, there were two main concerns with the school's existing dress code. First, it listed disciplinary action *before* the guidelines. This immediately signaled a negative undertone that the dress code was responded to punitively rather than as a learning experience. Compliance was the expectation. However, the most effective and motivating educators are those who do not force students to comply. Instead, they help students understand that there is value in something, and to take part in it in a way that has longer lasting impact **[AU: Please clarify what you mean by this.]**. The dress code was written in a way that suggested the school had to use force to foster compliance from students.

Second, the first requirements listed in the existing dress code were obviously directed toward female students, and the position at the beginning of the list suggested that the female requirements were the most important, primary dress code issues: "Clothing must cover the front and the back of the student (off-the-shoulder tops, tops with spaghetti straps, bare midriffs, halter tops, and tank tops are not permitted)," and "Shorts or skirts must not be too short or too tight fitting."

Here was opportunity for buy-in, the reason to steal: The school district in Oregon does an excellent job of maintaining that a dress code is necessary but that it must be fair and sensible. Students should recognize the value of the dress code and in fact, take part in determining what is appropriate. Safety, inoffensive wording, and gender-neutral descriptions of length, size, and so on are prerequisites to a fair and equitable dress code for all. The dress code was revised, liberated from any gender-specific phrasing to foster a fair and equitable dress code, and the school community participated.

The new dress code uses language like: " . . . encourages all students to be able to dress comfortably for school without fear of punishment or disruption to their learning process." The importance here is that the learning process not be disrupted, a key tenet indicating that dress code should not be on par with serious disciplinary infractions. Additionally, the wording about size and fit broadly allows for discretion: "Basic Principle: Certain body parts must be covered for all students."

Dress codes should continue to maintain a standard of safety, prohibiting offensive language, and exposure of undergarments—all in gender-neutral language—as well as a respectful, nonoffensive standard. It is remarkable to consider how one small child influenced an entire school community, which is now a better place for it. Think about the influence you can have with some subtle yet significant shifts to the language in your school's own dress code.

Engage your school community and your students to manage longer-term acceptance of principles. This also creates a more harmonious relationship among staff and students. Remember that stealing from other school communities, sometimes prompted by the child you least expect, is another effective way to make your school a better, more equitable place for all.

INCREASE YOUR PTA ATTENDANCE BY A FACTOR OF FIFTEEN

PTA meetings are one of most schools' long-standing access points for educators and parents. Yet parents are busy running kids from here to there, taking care of their own life tasks, and working to support it all. Too often, we see the most supportive schools struggling to break double digits in PTA meeting attendance even though the typical school has hundreds, maybe thousands, of parents. This has been a challenge for decades in school communities, which have tried everything from raffles to guest speakers to hot-topic discussions to entice parents to attend.

Is the persistent problem of low PTA meeting attendance the result of apathy? One community discovered that disinterest in school involvement was a far cry from reality. Parents were interested in participating and wanted to be part of the community—yes, even PTA meetings. They just couldn't get there. So the school decided to stop trying to sell the meeting against the backdrop of life's competitive distractions. Instead, why not try to bring the meeting to the parents?

Technology offers remote accessibility to foster meetings for those at great distances. It can also serve to bring a community together when life gets in the way of driving, parking, sitting, and worrying about other day-to-day errands that were left undone. It's no wonder parents can't make it to yet another meeting. Here is how one school community solved this problem.

Using the community-wide call system, the school asked families to watch the meeting live using a link included in the message; this produced the kind of attendance that had not been seen for years. While there were 14 parents at the PTA meeting, 176 viewers watched the live broadcast. That means PTA meeting attendance effectively jumped from 1.1 percent to 14 percent, a twelvefold increase!

The next day, the school sent out a blast with the good news and another promotion: If parents didn't get to watch the meeting live, they could still see the meeting offline by clicking on the provided link. An additional 52 viewers watched offline, for a total of 228, or 18 percent of the school's parental population.

Eighteen percent attendance may sound low, but consider the historical proportion—an eighteenfold increase. These are purposeful professional development opportunities for parents and faculty. The school would rather see 18 percent than 1.1 percent attendance. The numbers continue to rise as parents become aware of the convenience and access to both live and offline viewing. They can watch right from their smartphones while they are standing in line at the supermarket.

If this has piqued your interest, you're going to want to replicate it as a quick microstrategy rather than spending hours and years trying to entice parents to your school building to see PTA meetings. Here's how:

Step 1: Sign up with a free livestreaming service such as YouTube. It's a well-known interface and most people have a Google account already.
Step 2: Go to the camera in the upper right-hand area of your YouTube browser and click on it.
Step 3: Select Go Live.
Step 4: Create a title for your viewers.

Step 5: Change Public to Unlisted.

Step 6: You can instantaneously prepare to broadcast live. YouTube will prompt you for an image and take one at a 3-2-1 countdown. I recommend holding up a school emblem or just smiling nicely.

Step 7: Click Next.

Step 8: Connect to the school network from any device with a camera to broadcast.

Step 9: You can share a unique link to your livestream. Just click the three dots on the lower-right part of the screen and select Share.

Step 10: You're live! If you want, you can schedule live broadcasts and grab the link earlier.

This is not just for administrators. Think about many events educators can use streaming services. Examples include streaming for professional development, night events like a World Languages event invitation to the community, and use by special permission to broadcast with and for your students within a class. One word of caution: Remember that you must have permission to film and broadcast students. Ensure that you protect student privacy at all costs.

Bringing meetings to people makes sense. We're all busy running from here to there. Let your families watch from the comfort of their home, in a supermarket line, or wherever they may be. Also offer them the choice of when to view the meeting. Technology allows for this, and families appreciate the access.

ZEN DEN FOR IMPROVING EVERYONE'S WELLNESS IN YOUR SCHOOL

We have established that anxiety is rising among children as well as teachers. It may be that school communities are just beginning to recognize anxiety as a problem for children and the adults working with them. Regardless, we know the problem exists. While schools should do well to address morale among their faculty and provide supports for children in crisis, conventional methods can only go so far. For instance, counseling supports, parent conferences, and assemblies are all helpful, but schools must do more.

Recognizing that anxiety has a direct impact on the wellness of school communities enables us to help children and faculty manage their day-to-day challenges. Stealing ideas to help address this is prudent, because like any microstrategy, it saves time to borrow ideas, modifying them if necessary to fit your school community. That's why this section serves to encourage you to "copy and paste" the ideas you see here, which are already effectively being used as innovative solutions.

Anxiety affects everything from student performance to school safety. Utilizing tools to tackle anxiety head-on is not only a good idea, it will help your school climate and performance as well as the mental health of individuals in your community. One simple way to do this is with the use of wellness rooms. One school called it the Zen Den.

A wellness room—like the Zen Den adopted at this school—is an area designed to help students (and, separately, faculty) under duress to literally rewire their brains. Below are some basic steps the school outlines to implement the Zen Den. By changing the brain through wellness, students, staff, and the entire community will see a vast improvement in their ability to tackle the daily challenges they are confronted with.

Students who struggle with regulating their emotions while facing the rigors of academic and social pressure at school often end up enduring disciplinary consequences for their outbursts. You see this when kids blow their top, cursing, threatening, or in some way demonstrating an irrational reaction, causing schools to respond in the only way they know how: using the institutional methods schools have invoked for generations.

This is not the fault of schools. They are given limited options, often governed by board policy or expectations set by those with limited understanding of the complex challenges students encounter every day. What if we could proactively reduce—or better yet, eradicate —these behaviors with an option that allows students to reset before they go too far? This is the purpose of wellness rooms like the Zen Den.

When you walk into the Zen Den, you practically forget you are in a school. The unknowing person might mistake this room for a spa. Playing in the background is soft, melodic, comforting music. In the air is a pleasant and soothing scent. Around the room are soft, comfortable chairs. On a table sit some nutritious goodies. Games invite the visitor to consider having competitive fun. Indeed, this room transforms the mindset of the visitor just as the room is transformed from the traditional classroom environment. Following is a description of what each of them might look like.

Student Zen Den

Pulling together resources within the school community and with some grant-funded help, you can create a safe space for students needing to release stress, reduce anxiety, and get refocused, just like this school did. The Zen Den enables students to decompress in ways that foster their readiness and willingness to return to the classroom refocused and rejuvenated. Following is a list of items housed in our Zen Den. You can try your own layout, just make it a place where students can quiet their mind.

Suggested Items for Your Student Zen Den:

- bean bags
- spider bungee chairs
- motivational posters
- mindfulness wall with activities/suggestions (positive self-talk affirmations, journaling, guided imagery, progressive muscle relaxation, mindful meditation, breathing techniques)
- lava lamps
- sound machine
- fish tank
- balls that expand and other tactile devices
- stress balls
- yoga poses poster
- activity/art therapy
- carpet

Faculty Zen Den

Faculty wellness is gradually becoming recognized as more critical to the long-term health and wellness of both the adults and the students they are charged with teaching. That's because a well-balanced adult is a far more impactful teacher than an unwell one. Think about your worst, most dreadful days, perhaps when you have had too little sleep or are distracted by a crisis in your personal life. Are you as focused and prepared for the challenges children bring on those days? Can you manage and even help the child in need while you are under your own personal pressures? Obviously not, and schools would be wise to equip teachers with the resources and outlets to find their own place to quiet their mind. As a matter of fact, just offering such a resource in schools is a psychological advantage: Often, knowing we have this resource at our disposal doesn't mean we are inclined to use it, but the comfort we take in its accessibility is inarguable. Following is a list of items you might like to consider when fashioning your own faculty wellness room.

Suggested Items for Your Faculty Zen Den:

- couch
- antigravity lounge chairs
- book shelf with shared books—give a book, take a book
- framed quotes
- table lamp
- soft music
- quote on the wall
- soft carpet

A word of caution: You may be confronted by some pushback from either your community or some of your faculty who believe that these support systems are hokey. They may push the belief that we are not as tough as we used to and students have a responsibility to fulfill their academic requirements and "toughen up," a zen den could appear to someone with this view as an unnecessarily excessive luxury. Yet students and adults both perform better when offered supports that provide outlets.

My counter to this is always: Okay, maybe we should be tougher. Maybe kids should fulfill their academic requirements [AU: again—shouldn't they? Isn't the counter not that they shouldn't have to, but that the Zen Den actually helps them do so?]. As nostalgic as this may sound, this approach is not realistic. We know this from being in schools long enough to observe that mental breakdowns can put school officials, parents, and students on a destructive path, and it is time to stop ignoring the benefits of wellness supports.

You might anticipate some of the challenges characterized before rolling out a wellness room, so be proactive. Share the research with your community. Engage faculty in professional development. Bring guest speakers in who have direct experience with students and adults who fall prey to mental breakdowns. Even consider sharing tragic circumstances, like the school shootings that have become too much a part of our security discussions, not to scare but to share the reality of why it makes sense to acknowledge and embrace supports like a Zen Den.

CHAPTER SUMMARY

1. *Hands Up!* Rather than yelling at or pleading with students for their attention when engrossed in technology, implement this simple strategy, which removes students' tactile attention from the computer screen and swiftly draws their attention to you.
2. *Dress Code Dilemmas: How One Small Child Can Change a School.* Sometimes the most sensible decision a school official can make is to listen to the students, especially when rules have become archaic. Use other schools' movements to proactively permit student choice that empowers fair and equitable treatment among your school community.
3. *Increase Your PTA Attendance by a Factor of Fifteen.* Stop fighting an uphill battle and embrace technology to bring PTA meetings to your parents rather than being frustrated by low attendance. One school did this and increased attendance eighteenfold.

4. *Zen Den for Improving Everyone's Wellness in Your School.* Create a quiet, mindful place for students and adults alike to recharge so they can return to the classroom in a more productive, focused, and healthy mindset.

Chapter Seven

The Importance of the 80/20 Principle of Management

With the inevitable day-to-day challenges educators face, the added stress caused when something prevents you from doing your best exhausts the most well-intentioned educators. It is important to recognize our own locus of control; that is, what we have control over versus what is beyond our control. Too often, battles are fought on moral grounds. Debating for moral purposes can be defended as a strong belief of such issues.

It is human nature to dig in with primal fight or flight tactics, yet maneuvering on smarter ways often helps us focus on and achieve the end goal, which must always be to help children succeed. When faced with such unavoidable challenges, it is cost prohibitive and a waste of resources to fight such overwhelming hurdles to achieve your goal. Understanding this premise and recognizing the concept of the 80/20 principle will not only get you to your goal of helping children succeed, it will also inspire you to regain control of the very thing you are trying to achieve.

The 80/20 principle holds that we can maintain control over only approximately 80 percent of our world, whether it's at work, in the supermarket line, driving in a car, or in a hotly contested argument. Understanding this and embracing that 80 percent is far more effective than getting stuck in the 20 percent. These stumbling blocks are most often associated with bureaucracy deeply engrained in the system or are due to a leader who fails to recognize the value of the concept, vision, or goal.

The smartest solution is ultimately to recognize a larger set of options and be willing to adjust to achieve our goals. Think about the time consumed with fighting the establishment. Not only does it typically frustrate you, but worse, you most often still don't reach your end goal. We must view achieving success by working around an obstacle that's in our way rather than confronting, and in the process, save critical time and resources with the 80/20 microstrategy.

Let us examine several real-life examples of ways educators have utilized the 80/20 principle to save valuable time and meet their objectives. Grasping power from negative forces or people is one of the most significant ways to achieve this. We have all seen how life can be sucked out of an idea, or energy out of a creative educator, by one simple statement: "This won't work."

Every educator who has experienced this when trying to roll out an idea knows the devastating loss associated with it, the discomfort so great you might want to run out of the room! The maxim that you never directly challenge someone like this, especially in front of others, is correct, but that doesn't mean you give up or do nothing about it.

When confronted with energy vampires, it is important to remember that most professionals in education do not share the negative outlook that just a few seem to rent space in our heads with. That is power. How you engage professionals in an idea is as powerful. Rather than risk rolling out an idea that you know will likely be shot down by a negative person, start small, with positive, creative individuals. Seek these individuals out privately and protect them. Build on the success of their talents and energy and then demonstrate this so that the energy vampire in the room is confronted with indisputable evidence.

These are incremental and powerful ways to usurp the negative person's power. Remember that this convincing evidence is far more powerful than our attempts to argue with difficult opposers. With the 80/20 principle, it is not only a good idea but necessary to understand that these attempts by negative people are not personal. No, it is unlikely that they are throwing you under the bus; in fact, in a strange twist, these individuals may be looking to protect you from what they perceive is certain failure! Although their approach is not helpful, they do not see it that way. Empower yourself by remembering that 80 percent of this is how you perceive it—which choice will you make?

MANAGING OUR GOOD INTENTIONS TO SHIFT TOWARD SUCCESS

A school leader set out to address the needs of her school community and therefore to utilize some of her resources to address student needs. Recognizing the ever-increasing number of at-risk students, she saw a parallel rise in school security personnel. As the additional security staff members settled into the school community, she contemplated purposing her new human resources.

Her assistant principal was working on his final certification requirements needed to fulfill an action research project. This was the ideal opportunity. She charged him with developing a program that would embrace the school security personnel in ways that could help at-risk students.

The assistant principal created a dynamic program that the school referred to as a Schoolhouse Adjustment. The premise was simple: Students were referred to the school resource officer (SRO) in lieu of a first-time suspension or to accompany a lesser disciplinary consequence. The SRO met with the child during an available class or free period, depending on the student's schedule.

A brief summary of the infraction was presented to the SRO. Accompanying this was a sample guide with corresponding activities that were geared toward a focus on prevention in the future, rather than punishment for the past. The SRO was trained for the program and also drew from his prior law enforcement experience.

This program met with magnificent success. Suspension rates dropped by one-third, in large part due to this new program. Student behavior and the school climate improved. This was a win-win. The school succeeded in tackling a major challenge: how to reduce behaviors that obstructed student learning by an increasing at-risk population. The program even made the education news, with a publication describing its success! Seems like a no-brainer, right?

There was one problem lurking behind all this success: The central office administrator who oversaw school security in the district questioned the validity of the program. He was himself a strong administrator, but also strong willed. The principal and school security personnel repeatedly showed the central office administrator the facts, and the results were virtually indisputable. However, he had what he felt were larger concerns: He felt as though the program took security away from their duties.

The principal could argue that school security personnel were in fact enhancing security measures in ways that cannot be quantified by building important relationships with at-risk students. But whether the principal agreed with the administrator's concerns was irrelevant. What mattered was that over time, the central office administrator continued to question the value of pulling a school resource officer away from security matters to work one-on-one with children.

This may sound as ludicrous as it is to write about. What better way to increase security than through building relations with children who were most at risk? It didn't matter. The administrator had made up his mind, and he was, after all, the principal's superior. He arrived at the school one day, and in no uncertain terms made clear his expectation that in only one small circumstance was the principal authorized to enlist SROs to engage at-risk students: if there was a police report associated with the referral. This directly contradicted the philosophy behind the program to provide an intervention in lieu of or reduction of a consequence in order to reach at-risk students. And with that, this program, in essence, was ended.

Or was it? After all that had been invested in this program and the evidence of its benefit to the school, was it worth throwing it all away? Perhaps the principal could charge into the superintendent's office or engage news outlets to protest the central office administrator's uncompromising position in a Hail Mary effort to restore this program. But school politics don't work like the fairy-tale ending in a movie. The reality was that the levels of bureaucracy would, at a minimum, hinder the rejuvenation of this program, and at worst eliminate it altogether—all due to backlash from a potentially unhappy central office administrator armed with the strength of position and district-wide respect. This program was on a cataclysmic path.

The end goal in any 80/20 situation is the objective. Proving you are right or that someone else is wrong is not in calibration with this microstrategy. So this principal responded in a way that was far more effective. She looked at the cinder-block wall in her office and thought for a moment before responding to the assistant superintendent's ultimatum: *If I argue and fight this cause, it may be less comfortable then banging my head against that wall. Worse, what would it be worth?*

The chance of overturning the edict presented as much risk as the long-term damage done to the hierarchical relationship she was engaged in with her superior. Yet the loss of the program was nothing short of devastating. The principal's 20 percent lack of control felt much larger in this moment: Argue the 20 percent and spend a lot more time and aggravation, all the while not likely reversing any decision. Her response may be surprising, but read on to find out why.

"No problem," she replied.

Looking somewhat surprised, the assistant superintendent asked, "So, we are good?"

"We are good." The principal smiled, flashing a thumbs up.

The central office administrator backed out of the room in disbelief at how easy this conversation went for him. The next day, the principal called her assistant principal and several staff members into a meeting, announcing that due to unforeseen circumstances, the Schoolhouse Adjustment program was no longer in existence. But she announced, "This is an opportunity to make a similar program, even bigger and better!"

Bigger and better indeed. What transpired was a transformation of the program, a method that expanded the current system, shifting from two SROs accepting recommended student candidates to five teachers. Each had various prep period times available, so together they were available at different points in the day to work with the recommended student candidates. They embraced the program as vested positive behavior support staff. No longer were there restrictions on the program imposed by the smaller SRO staff and more limited availability, and there was more—something surprising happened.

This principal had always thought that SROs, typically retired police officers, would be ideal for the Schoolhouse Adjustment project. To some degree, this was true—their law enforcement background gave students a different perspective than what teachers can offer. Yet law enforcement personnel are militant in their style, personality, and approach, something that goes only so far with most students. Others needed a kind hand, a loving or nurturing mentor, and that is what these teachers could offer, and where the program's benefits expanded even further.

This kind of relationship building matches the benefits of and crosses over into key mentoring relationships students gain from adults. This is hugely beneficial to at-risk children, who are often exposed to trauma and lack critical resources and the support of adults at their side when they need guidance. These students can be helped through distressing experiences with the safeguard from mentors at school.

Mentoring gives at-risk children opportunities, experiences, and hope that would likely be otherwise unavailable to them. After all, isn't a concept like mentoring, which helps children have supports in place to help them grow what is at the very core of those who embrace growth mindset to achieve success? These students are in dire need of positive, nonpunitive mentors and teachers to provide them support and afford them opportunities that they would otherwise not have access to.

At-risk children who enjoy the benefits of a mentor often show greater likelihood of success in life. They demonstrate the ability to further their education. These children are more likely to give back to society in adulthood; in turn, they may help others avoid the path of destructive behaviors. These children even have the capacity to take on leadership positions.

The advantage of using teachers vested in positive behavior support was apparent in their caring, instructional approach to students. These teachers know the qualities of a good lesson. Teachers know that relationship building, empathy, and intrigue are critical components of an effective instructional technique. SROs would know this only if they possessed an intuitive sense that their training did not necessarily provide or enhance. The advantage was clear, and the results even more far-reaching.

This principal learned an important lesson in the 80/20 principle. When you are fighting the uphill battle of the 20 percent you cannot control, you quickly exhaust your energy, creativity, and achievement. Focusing on the 80 percent fosters creativity and empowerment. The results are even better. This principal has successfully developed her new model program, called Restorative Service Program (RSP), and other schools are adopting it. That's invention by accident!

Chapter 7

CLOWN SHOES

It is easy to take over in a new job when a prior educator was not well liked or had checked out long before retirement. The real challenge is when we enter into an opportunity and literally replace a legend. This can be true in any domain in education: replacing a retired teacher, an outgoing coach, or an administrator.

Understanding that we have little control over the perceptions of others and that we must instead focus on ourselves and our own abilities frees us from the shackles of proving we are as good as the legend we are replacing, even when others hold on to the past. Let's look at a case and learn how one educator overcame that burden.

Having taught special education, Sean felt well-equipped to take on this new assignment as an assistant principal. He left his position as a teacher in one middle school to accept the opportunity in another middle school. Sean faced interesting challenges, like Melissa, who would leave her room regularly to make personal phone calls in the teacher lounge during class time. Concerned about her negligence, Sean questioned Melissa, to which she replied, "I have been teaching longer than you have been alive." But that wasn't the most daunting hurdle he faced. No, that hurdle appeared, large and overwhelming, on the first day at his new school.

Eager and full of energy, the new assistant principal entered his office. Having taught for only four years before being thrust into this new opportunity as an assistant principal, Sean had big shoes to fill; he knew that. The previous assistant principal Oscar was so popular and well respected, even the mayor attended his farewell party! Oscar had a strong respect and naturally commanded respect from the entire school community. So on his first day, on Sean's desk, he found a great big pair of clown shoes.

Somewhat perplexed, Sean picked up these out-of-place clown shoes to see what was going on. Underneath sat a small, very subtle but neatly written note, with a memorable line that he would never forget: "Good luck, you've got big shoes to fill!" Taking a deep breath, Sean thought about the challenges that lay ahead, never truly able to comprehend all that was the monumental challenge before him as a young and naive new administrator.

The shoes Sean had to fill certainly were massive. Worse, Oscar was still serving as the principal of a neighboring school, where he was promoted to the next phase of his career. Oscar's legend would live on as this new administrator stood in that large shadow.

Sean decided he could never live up to that outgoing administrator. In fact, he should not even try. Sean needed to find his own way, with his own style and personality. Sean set out over the next five years to do just that. He learned along the way. There were challenges, like the union leader teacher who made tasks daunting. But after months of union leadership questioning every decision Sean made, one day in the spring, the union leader shut his door on excessively late students who had been repeatedly warned about arriving to class late, after the bell.

These students came to the new assistant principal to complain about the door being shut. They explained, "We weren't even that late this time, maybe a minute." The assistant principal responded, "If I were you, I'd hurry back there and promise him you'll never do it again, because you'll be lucky to face his discipline instead of mine."

Later that day, the union leader came to Sean's office, stood at the door, and, as Sean looked up, winked and said thanks with a smile. It was the first time this teacher had smiled or acknowledged Sean's efforts. It wasn't the last. That day, he learned that of the hundreds of interactions he had everyday, this was one of the small but significant ones. It was the difference, a defining moment in how he made his own way.

Five years later, at a going-away party for this assistant principal thrown by his staff, the former assistant principal—the one whose legendary status had seemed so beyond his skill set—sat proudly looking on at him while the faculty wished him farewell. He was grateful to have his predecessor's support and presence there because it gave him the opportunity to thank him. It also gave him the chance to have a little fun.

When he stood up to make his farewell speech, he brought out those great big clown shoes. He fondly thanked his predecessor before noting that "you left something behind in my office—your shoes." Recalling the story for his staff and predecessor, it served as one of the most memorable experiences he had. It was an important example of recognizing what he had control over and what he did not. The 20 percent that revolved around the legendary status of the former administrator was beyond him. Focusing on the 80 percent empowered him to show what he could do with his own skill set—different, yes, but effective certainly—and in his own way.

STOPPING THE BULLY ON THE BUS

One of the most difficult management issues for schools is bus conduct because direct supervision by school officials cannot occur. In fact, imagine the scenario: A driver sits facing forward with more than fifty students behind him, virtually unsupervised, while he attempts to manage one of the largest and most difficult vehicles on the road. Naturally, as with a substitute teacher, some children take advantage of this.

Fortunately, most students only act a little silly or get a bit too loud, to which the driver tells them to "settle down," and they comply—at least for the moment. But sometimes the behavior of students gets out of hand, or is even appalling. In the worst-case scenarios, a bully takes advantage and the school must step in to stop the bullying. But what happens when parental and political pressure gets in the way of helping a victimized child? Let's explore one example and see how the administrator overcame these obstacles by applying the 80/20 principle.

Chase was quiet, polite, and a bit smaller than his peers. A student had been harassing Chase on the bus for months, and over time the building administrator issued progressive measures of discipline consistent with the school's code of conduct. This began with a warning, followed by detentions and short-term bus suspensions (removal from the bus). It seemed the more the school intervened, the more this child accelerated his behavior and targeted Chase.

This horrendous scenario was overshadowed by antagonistic parents who challenged the school's authority at every step and ignored their child's conduct. The building administrator would never forget meeting with the father of the victim one day or the tears in his eyes as he begged, "Why can't you stop the bullying?" The bully had victimized his son yet again, intimidating him, blocking his attempts to sit down, and cursing at him, all after repeated attempts to redirect his behavior. This was the last straw.

It was early April and there was still a full marking period remaining in the school year. The building administrator called the bully into his office after a week off the bus and, on a conference call (the parents refused to meet in person), warned him that if he bullied Chase again, he would be removed from the bus for the remainder of the school year. After arguing with this, the parents threatened that they would "go to the superintendent if you do that."

Immediately upon reentry to the bus, the child unrelentingly bullied Chase again, refusing to let him pass to his assigned seat and shouting names at him. What transpired was a chain of events that would be unbelievable to a logical person and would make the hair stand up on the back of your head.

The building administrator met with the student and his parents—this time, they came in person—and notified them that their child was suspended from the bus for the remainder of the year. Shouting and threatening the administrator with legal action, they charged over to the superintendent's office, and twenty minutes later the assistant superintendent of student services called the building administrator, demanding the child be returned to the bus.

The building administrator responded, "If you make me put this kid back on the bus, you can expect the same man who was crying in my office, asking me why I can't stop the bullying to be at a board meeting, and there may be press there too." With an aggravated tone, the assistant superintendent said, "All right, but you have to get him on another bus, and call the parent back to explain this to them!"

Still in shock, the building administrator contacted the supervisor of transportation and explained the scenario and the directive. The transportation supervisor found the closest bus passage and said, "Okay, I have an alternate option—oh, but wait, there is one problem."

The building administrator replied, "What's that?"

"This student's street is one mile long and the bus can only drop him off at the end because it's a dead end."

The building administrator knew this was legal; other students safely walked up to one and a half miles without a bus in this town. After a brief pause, he responded, "I don't see a problem with that. Do you see a problem with that?"

Following an equally brief pause, the transportation supervisor replied, "Oh, no, I don't see a problem with that either!" The administrator could almost see her smile through the phone.

The administrator contacted the parent of the bully, as directed, and notified him about the bus reassignment. The parent responded, "Thank you," and slammed the phone down.

Two days later, the administrator received a call from the parent, asking, "Did you know that the new bus drops my son off a mile from our house?"

He tried to put on his best astonished voice and responded, "Really? I didn't know that."

The bully's parent replied, "Yes, it is. I think I'm going to drive him to school for the rest of the year."

The administrator replied, in his best gentle tone, "I think that's a good idea." He hung up the phone with a smile that matched the transportation supervisor's on the day he spoke with her.

The 80/20 principle was applied here, not only in an effective fashion, but in one where the building administrator recognized his limits and played the game. So often, we have little or no control over political pressure that overrides the ethical value of an attempted action. Yet there are times—not always—when if we play our cards right, justice is still served.

This story may sound ludicrous—it should sound insane—but it is an all-too-real scenario in the political landscape of schools and parents and board votes. Understanding this and not letting it baffle you will help you sometimes—more often than you think—to win a battle for an innocent bullied victim, an at-risk child, or in many other scenarios where ethics should win out over politics.

THE BLINDSIDE PROJECT: IF YOU COULD DO IT BETTER BECAUSE YOU PUT YOUR PRIDE ASIDE, WOULD YOU?

Schools have limited budgets, and expensive commercial products are sold that claim to save the day. Yet everything about success, both in school and outside of it, is about relationships. In the face of adversity and obstacles, one school discovered that changing a child's scenario of a life of trouble gave the child an opportunity in spite of a disadvantage the school was confronted with.

It is a touching account of how a school community can come together to make the best of a challenging circumstance, one that in the end helped children on both sides of an issue. They chose to take a difficult situation and turn it around to a positive in a way that helped children in need.

If you have ever seen the movie *The Blindside*, you can appreciate that regardless of a child's upbringing, given the right conditions, he or she can succeed beyond all expectations. The premise of this story is that a child faced with horrendous, even nightmarish circumstances was able to come out of his shell and excel beyond anyone's wildest dreams. That's because, like so many facing these circumstances, that child possessed a beauty inside that was hidden until the right person helped open the door for him.

Schools can do this for children, but we must be creative, even unconventional. That is the purpose of a program begun at a suburban middle school with a fast-changing demographic of increasingly more at-risk children. Remarkably, this simple program has accomplished the goal of reaching children who do not receive the same nurturing in their lives that most children take for granted. This child and the other children affected had their lives changed forever because they faced down a daunting task and chose to make lemonade out of lemons.

To understand how this powerful program worked so effectively—not in spite of but because of its simplicity—you must first understand the conditions the school was under, and how the school community overcame some unexpected challenges that caused an almost unbearable dilemma. It is a program that is replicable, and it works far better than many of the expensive, complex commercial programs schools spend countless dollars on.

Early one spring, when the first flowers were peeking out at the warming sun, a middle school faced unexpected staffing cuts that were the most dramatic seen in more than a decade. But there was more. At the same time these cuts were being announced, the school learned it was to inherit the exploding preschool program, which had previously been housed in the eight elementary schools. Preschool kids in middle school? Yes, nearly two hundred of them!

It is human nature to feel angry, put upon, and mistreated when being dealt such a hand. Staffing cuts at the same time the school population would be increased by nearly 20 percent meant the remaining staff would be expected to do more with less. The school administration was charged with figuring this out, a process that normally takes weeks or months. They were given days to find a location in the school to house an additional two hundred preschool-aged children alongside the current growing roster of fourteen hundred middle schoolers. Facing this monumental challenge, one might expect the school officials to throw in the towel and cry "Uncle!" Then something magical happened: summer.

Summer is often a time of rest, relaxation, and reflection. This slower-paced season provides educators the opportunity to explore ways to make their schools better. This summer occurred right as these school officials thought of all the overwhelming changes they were confronted with. This is where the 80/20 principle most critically factors in: Make lemonade out of lemons, especially when it comes to helping kids in otherwise seemingly insurmountable circumstances. That is power and helps us to do better than trying to control a circumstance that seems insurmountable. We can be inspired by it.

Back to *The Blindside*. In the story, a family adopts the high school–aged homeless child named Michael. They see his kind and gentle heart and the incredible potential that exists inside him. This potential was ignored by many because he was, after all, from the wrong side of the tracks. This tragedy repeats itself in so many sad, somber stories of children deprived and unloved, left against all odds. It is no wonder they find attention in the only way they know how—attracting negative notice and consequences.

So begins the irreversible path of discipline that results in "bigger problems for bigger kids." More severe problems often lead to legal consequences, which doom the once-forgotten child to a life of loss, and the cycle repeats. It doesn't have to be this way, and we don't need to spend inordinate amounts of money to solve the problem. That's what happened at this school—and it's working, one child at a time. Still interested? Read on.

The amazing thing about kids is that they are sponges, ready to soak up just about anything they can get their hands on. If the options are negative, though, that's what they absorb. Reverse this by offering one option that literally rewires the brains of children, propelling them to realize their potential through simple acts of kindness: not punishment, but literally the complete opposite.

That's where the preschool kids come in. You can put almost any older child in a room with a cute puppy and what does the child do? Cuddle, pet, and love the puppy. This is so even for at-risk children, because they get love back. It's that simple. This "dog therapy" also works remarkably well with little kids.

A common teacher complaint heard by administrators is, "That child needs to receive consequences!" The teacher who says this is right, and we can offer consequences by offering a new solution.

Chris was a big kid, nearly six feet tall at the age of just thirteen, towering over kids and teachers alike. He had a nice smile, but teachers quickly saw past that as he raced down the hall, yelling and causing bedlam. It was easy to see why teachers wanted action, and action they got. The idea was to offer this child the chance to read to the preschool kids. Would he really go for it?

Teachers didn't believe it. He would *never* do that. He's too much trouble. He's too big. He's too this and he's too that.

When offered this option, he smiled, shrugged, and said, "Sure." He had to earn it: Good enough behavior for a period of time that he could leave class to go in and read to the little ones. He was at least two grade levels behind in reading and struggling academically. This was a big risk, but he earned his chance.

Chris was given three books to select from. He took them home, reviewed them, and selected the book he wanted to read: *Pete the Cat*. It was a story about realizing you are just fine being yourself. The irony was not lost on the adults in the room, watching him read proudly, his same giant smile no longer hidden by fear or expected disappointment. This was his moment.

The great thing about preschool-aged children is that they are "blind" to assumptions. They did not see Chris as a large, intimidating, and troubled presence. To them, he was a huggable, lovable young man who was sharing his time and offering a story they loved to hear from an older child. The connection was instant.

Chris returned to read holiday stories and more to the preschool class, and the program quickly expanded thanks to donors who rapidly bought into the concept. One hundred at-risk children are given the opportunity to participate. They select books, join the Middles to Littles program, and are anointed with an official T-shirt.

Teachers look at Chris differently since he became part of this program. That is half the battle. If he runs a little too fast or laughs a little too loud, they do not corner him and question his conduct. Instead, they practically put a nurturing arm around him and talk to him about doing the right thing, in a kind, even grandparently, way.

The children involved in this program carry themselves in a less defensive, combative posture. They express a sense of responsibility to something larger than themselves. This feeling of altruism is free advertising—it's a lot less expensive than adopting some new and expensive commercial products. Remember that this is a low-cost program, effective, and, best of all, reproducible.

If you don't have a preschool program accessible to you, bring the kids to you via video conference or bus students to nearby schools, if possible. Videoconferencing has worked with ill children who want to be part of the program as well. Try your own Middles to Littles microstrategy. Remember that when you face a daunting challenge, you take control of that 80 percent when you choose to make lemonade out of lemons. That's power to make real change, despite the challenges surrounding us.

CHAPTER SUMMARY

1. *Managing Our Good Intentions to Shift Toward Success.* When bureaucracy stands in your way and you know a good idea is evaporating, don't lose momentum by fighting an impossible uphill battle. Rather, embrace the challenge and invent a successful alternative, something that could match or even increase the success of the original idea.
2. *Clown Shoes.* When you replace someone in an assignment who was well respected, do not try to replicate what your predecessor did. Find your own way and stand by your identity. Eventually, everyone will come along and believe in you for who you are, not who you are trying to be.
3. *Stopping the Bully on the Bus.* School officials are always trying to balance the tension between effectively managing their school and the political landscape in which school communities often reside. When politics overrides ethics, school officials get understandably upset with the dynamic, but if they play their cards right, they can win ethical victories more often than they may think.
4. *The Blindside Project: If You Could Do It Better Because You Put Your Pride Aside, Would You?* When life brings you lemons, make lemonade, especially when it comes to helping kids. Embrace the challenges you are presented and gain back control to make the lives of kids and their school life better.

Chapter Eight

Getting Your School/Classroom to Perform Its Best in "Flow"

Flow is a concept that refers to being in the zone. We have all had the experience of feeling flow, and it most often occurs randomly, unplanned, and unknowingly. What if we could harness this flow source for enhanced and more sustained productivity and optimal performance in our schools and classrooms? Organizational and individual flow have gained attention over recent years, and channeling energy into a flow state is an attractive approach to the success of an individual or organization.

Schools and educators can benefit from finding to consider ways to impact their organizational and individual flow. Flow conditions can be happening randomly but structuring for conditions to stimulate flow can be rooted in a more planned, and optimized manner. Following are several simple yet powerful methods to concentrate flow in schools and classrooms.

HOW ONE SCHOOL SAVED EIGHT SCHOOL DAYS

You don't have to get everyone on board to save eight valuable school days. That's right: While many in education are looking to save minutes, one school figured out how to save *days* over the course of a school year. It didn't require getting everyone to fall in line, either. As in so many instances, when this school pushed to save time, there was some resistance. Yet the majority—more than 90 percent of staff and students—embraced the concept. Here's how it worked and how you can apply a similar strategy in your class or school to save precious instructional time and increase student achievement.

If your school or classroom is like most, clearing the halls and getting students into their classrooms on time can be a monumental challenge. When students move between classes during transitions, a bell signals their departure and arrival. The time between the official end of one class and the beginning of the next seems simple enough, but students often use this time for social interactions instead.

Whether the school is small and moves on a short bell schedule of two to three minutes or is larger, requiring a transition of four to five minutes, students often delay their initial arrival to class primarily for social reasons. Therefore, the real cost is lost time after classes start, which affects everything from student learning, time on task, focus, and school atmosphere. Often, the students most in need of starting the learning process on time are those wandering aimlessly right when learning is most pivotal.

It can be surprising how sluggishly students arrive to class, and worse, how lethargic teachers are at teaming up in the hallways to make student arrival time a factor of accountability for their classrooms. Students in the hall can create discipline issues and disrupt other classes, and disciplinary issues often accelerate among these transitions. Even if some students are seated and ready to go at the bell, the late arrival of other students—sometimes in a grandstanding fashion, announcing, "I'm here!"—disrupts the flow of all learners. One school decided to try something new, something competitive: hall races.

Impact of Time on Task

Teachers at this school tried to plead with and direct kids to comply with bell times, but to no avail. Concerned about lost time, the school started by collecting information to understand the lost time scenarios.

Confirming the concern, the school found the average start time was approximately 2.5 minutes *after* the bell sounded. This was a significant loss of instructional time for students, whose class periods are scheduled for forty-two minutes. This was unacceptable. Calculating this out across eight daily class periods in a year of 180 school days meant nearly 8 school days were lost. Here's how the numbers break down:

Eight periods daily = 336 minutes total instructional time; 2.5 minutes lost per class change = 15 minutes per day. 15 minutes lost per day = 1 full school day lost day every 24 days. This means on a 180-day calendar, 7.5 days of instruction time lost, forever! Something had to be done.

There Is a Solution

The school felt compelled to act in the face of this enormous loss of time. A solution, a fix that would be felt school-wide, had to be found. After exploring some options and reviewing previous failed attempts (efforts to enforce with students by way of negative consequences), the school started by doing a baseline study for a week where someone—an administrator, teacher on duty, or security—measures the average time it takes for the halls clear. While gathering this data, do not direct students to their classes, a difficult reality but necessary to access real-time data.

The school shifted to a positive approach by heavily promoting hall races as part of the schoolwide positive behavior support program. It was worth a shot to get kids to class. Each hallway competes against all the other hallways in the building. Whichever hallway is cleared first wins and are especially incentivized to be cleared before the bell to start the next class (double rewards for beating the bell). Hall races save an average of about 2.5 minutes per class period, and this results in a savings of nearly eight days of instructional time.

What better way to get students focused and engaged early in the class period? Hall races are conducted between classes throughout the day and vary from day to day. This allows halls, classrooms, and teachers an opportunity to incentivize students and staff during different stages and transitions of the day. Hall areas and their associated classes who win are awarded lottery tickets.

How It Changed the School

Students consistently arrive to class on time or within seconds of the final bell, encouraged by the possibility that there is a hall race under way and the expectation that students do not wander halls at this school. Teachers can get classes started sooner, avoid disruptions, and deal with less disruptive activity in the halls. Everyone has bought in to this win-win situation. The entire culture of the school has changed, and students are in classrooms far earlier than before, with nearly eight school days saved. This is one simple way to maximize learning and improve school climate.

This Can Work In Your School Too

You don't have to have a comprehensive positive behavior support system in place to employ this kind of positive reinforcement. The point is, make it about "winning." Students and faculty alike are inspired by the competitive edge. They see it as a positive energy contest. Students and faculty respond. Try it in your school and see how many days you get back!

MICROPD FOR A BETTER FLOW IN YOUR SCHOOL

Most schools have structures in which teachers and school counselors meet weekly to discuss grade level, team, or department progress of their students. Teachers and counselors can all become energy depleted—tasked with helping students achieve and dealing with the diverse challenges of students and parents—and even disenfranchised, witnessing slow progress for the most at-risk and time-consuming students. These setbacks or standstills seem to force us backward, and absence of visible growth is discouraging and can make us feel sluggish.

At the beginning of the year, when we are euphoric and well rested, looking forward to helping all our students, school teams often establish SMART goals (https://www.advancementcourses.com/blog/smart-goals) and meeting protocols (https://www.schoolreforminitiative.org/protocols/). These are ways to establish a system to reach our goals. As the year drags on and educators are looking over their shoulder at the high-pressure demands of preparing students for standardized testing, managing behavior issues, and more, this can feel overwhelming. The result can be that even the most positive teacher can feel less than enthusiastic. Against this seemingly insurmountable backdrop, there is a way to revitalize teachers: MicroPD!

It is generally accepted that professional development (PD) must go deeper than the one-and-done workshop. To do teacher PD right, it must be more sustained and more relevant, offering tangible takeaways. Recurring PD sessions tend to be informative, offer innovative takeaways, and elicit teacher input. Therefore, teachers generally enjoy them. However, as the year drags on, something more is needed—something different and stimulating.

The impact of short bursts of rejuvenating practices depends on the premise of mini sessions called MicroPD. These are five- to eight-minute invigorating opportunities for teachers to benefit from a practice that helps them bond. Think of this like an infusion to help teachers through the hard parts.

Here is how it works:

1. Introduce the concept: "Today, we're going to try something reenergizing, since it's midyear and we're all struggling with ongoing student problems, difficult parents, etc."
2. Read a team-building quote and have teachers reflect on it for thirty seconds to a minute.
3. Next, ask each team member to share how the quote applies to his or her team.
4. Last, share your own contribution.

Does it work? Not only do teachers enjoy the experience, but it truly uplifts them, empowering them through bonding. They jump right into the rest of the meeting with energy, humor, and creativity. Optimal energy and focus are what makes teams creative, something necessary during the more challenging parts of the day or the year. This simple, easy-to-replicate practice can occur regularly. The person facilitating the meeting can include some fun ideas, such as teachers offering their own innovative idea to their colleagues among other inspiring approaches.

You can end the meeting with something interesting and/or positive that was experienced, too. It doesn't have to be related to school—just something worthy of sharing. This reinforces the bonding experience critical for teamwork and collaboration. We are not so distant from each other when we learn something distinctive about and from each other. Colleagues can learn something new. In one instance, pairs of teachers realized they were running in the same marathon in the spring!

MicroPD is a quick and reenergizing way to bond faculty right before they go back into their classrooms to teach their students. What better ingredient can be infused into our focus for increasing instruction and learning? There is nothing more powerful than teachers sharing with their colleagues. It is at the foundation of every successful team, and students win as a result of refreshed, happy teachers.

SETTING THE TONE AT THE SCHOOLHOUSE DOOR

One of the best assets public schools enjoy is the opportunity to separate political agendas and religious affiliations from the democratic spirit of diversity. This allows classrooms to neutralize the antagonistic and counterproductive processes often riddling political and religious differences. Microaggressions resulting from these are damaging to all. School culture is negatively impacted, and the problems posed by microaggressions are detrimental to the school's culture and other organizations, impacting the productivity and performance of the school in undeniable ways.

When the ability for students to excel is interfered with by microaggressions, there is no dispute about the damage. Therefore, it is critical for schools and classrooms to recognize the destructive nature of microaggressions and polarization and take a proactive stance to flip the script and sustain this reversal through active monitoring. What follows is one effective and simple microstrategy to do this.

Every school has a main entrance. This location should be considered not just a physical entrance but also a symbolic doorway into the cultural beliefs of those who enter into the school. It is a focal point that should be embraced as a location to feature the clear cultural values of the school. Consider this an opportunity to advertise at the most visible location of your school. First impressions allow for a gateway into the expected behavior of those in the school: students, teachers, parents, and visitors alike.

One school displayed this on a large poster with bold lettering at the only security entrance authorized by the school for all students, staff, parents, and other visitors enter and exit through. The statement was simple yet powerful, establishing a clear value system that reinforced the school culture. This system created a barrier to outside forces that felt impenetrable. Here is this power statement:

> In this school, we speak over 67 languages, represent over a dozen races, ethnicities, and religious faiths. Together, we make one school, rich in tolerance and diversity. When you walk through these doors, you do so knowing there is no racism, bias, or bullying accepted in our school. Become a part of respect and tolerance and join our school community by entering now.

Educators who wish to make a statement representing a strong value system like this should embrace it, or a similar one, to make obvious to entrants the expectations inside the schoolhouse walls. Remember, too, that schoolhouse walls are represented in the "school zone." The school zone includes buses to and from school, bus stops, field trips off campus, and everywhere the school is present. Advertise in these arenas as well.

TRIVIA GAMES: GETTING TEAMS TO BOND RATHER THAN FIGHT

The organizations with the most talent are, unfortunately, not always the most successful. Think of a talented professional sports team, talked up as the team to beat due to all its talent, that doesn't live up to expectations. Was their talent misread? The answer is resoundingly no! The talent is there; it is impressive, premier, upper echelon. So what happened? Why do so many of the most talented teams stumble so miserably?

The answer is plainly pride. When pride gets in the way, individuals working together cannot gel. They cannot coordinate and often ignore each other's best ideas. The multiplier effect of successful teams is real, and the concept is straightforward. Accepting each other's ideas as viable possibilities frees up the creative channels of exploration and discovery. The multiplier perpetuates a synergistic effect that the team utilizes to make less-talented individuals a far more effective group when connected.

So how do we overcome the pride factor that so often creates the barrier enveloping the creative potential within team chemistry? The answer is simple, a solution that is both efficient and effective. When teams are arguing, disagreeing, playing one-up, and throwing each other under the bus, destructive forces are at work that must be reversed with quickness and force. To do this, it is important to first understand that this is not the fault of any one individual, regardless of how easy it is to be fooled into believing the appearance that one or two negative forces are causing this energy drain. Rather, the responsibility falls squarely on the shoulders of the leader.

The leader can be an administrator, a coach, or even the team facilitator or department head. Whoever this person is, he or she can and must lead the change. A simple, efficient, and effective tool for doing this was introduced by a principal who subsequently modeled it for others, and the tool has been adopted by many since then.

In this scenario, a special education team consisted of a school psychologist, a department chair, a social worker, and an emotional support teacher. Conflict between strong personalities, specifically the school psychologist and emotional support teacher, actually resulted in these two reporting what each perceived as ethical issues to the administrators.

It got so bad that at one point a disenfranchised student told the school psychologist that the special educator put another child in the class in a headlock, which the adult reported to the principal, demanding the principal invoke a formal investigation and child welfare referral. Instead, the principal called the alleged victim to his office, and this student quickly discredited the allegation. Rather than lecture the school psychologist about jumping to conclusions and false allegations, the principal did something unexpected, and this altered the trajectory of the toxic team within minutes.

Like other microstrategies shared throughout this book, this one can be applied to any team, in any circumstance, at any level, to correct destructive teamwork. The principal asked the department chair if he could try something unique and unexpected at the next department meeting. Desperate to attempt anything that might work, the chair said, "Sure, what do we have to lose?"

The principal arrived with a half-dozen folded scraps of paper and asked each member to write something interesting about themselves on the paper, then fold it and hand it back. He shuffled these and randomly handed them back to the group members. The rules, he announced, were simple: Read the interesting fact out loud and try to guess who the person was.

An idea like this may sound simple, common, and even childish. Yet wasn't that the very behavior occurring on this team? The principal was sincere in his reasoning for this activity and modeled reading and guessing, then the others in the group followed. Within five minutes, everyone was laughing, identifying each other and recognizing that their peers were people with stories just like their own.

Remember, this is the same group that was throwing each other under the bus only days earlier. This activity provided a reminder of what must always come first: that we are people with lives and sensitivities that must be brought to the fore or we will make inaccurate assumptions about each other and our intentions. This strategy has been used dozens of times by individuals who learned about it since, and it has been met with remarkably successful and sustainable results.

Sometimes the most obvious thing is also the hardest to see until we take the lead to arrange it. Leaders must take the lead in order to care for teams and do so with vigor. If you don't put your beliefs out in front of your faculty, they will make assumptions, and these assumptions are almost always inaccurate interpretations of the truth.

Be obvious, model, and look to build off the bonds between individuals, both naturally and through your own work when necessary. Individuals on a team must respect each other and decide that their work together is more important than their individual pride. They only see this when they also see each other. Pride blinds us, and we must push our teams to visualize success by pushing past pride.

CREATING FLOW IN FACULTY MEETINGS: THE "UN-FACULTY" MEETING

Faculty meetings can be dreadful. Anyone who has ever stood in an auditorium filled with tired-looking faculty after a long day of teaching knows the discomfort associated with this. Consider the paradox: Teachers are expected to sit and focus during their lowest energy cycle of the day. It is no wonder that—as with kids—we see distractibility, disinterest, and frustration.

It doesn't have to be this way. Absenteeism at one school spiked to 10 percent on faculty-meeting Mondays, more than double the average faculty absentee rate. Absent teachers make learning harder, and kids are in greater need of a positive and present adult influence in school more than ever.

So what can be done? The answer is surprisingly simple and sure to shift teachers into greater flow states to enhance their own professional development: Draw on research on effective professional learning communities for creation of a PLC model (All Things PLC, n.d.). Wrap this around a focus on learning and results with timely and relevant information. This can be accomplished no matter whether your faculty is large or small.

A model for any school, department, or grade level is one that breaks the process into parts as the key factor in executing the road map. Breaking the process into parts is the key factor in executing a road map. Here's how it works in one scenario, which is easily transferable to any school: Four administrators oversee eight departments (language arts, math, social studies, science, world languages, arts, technology, and physical education/health). You can facilitate with a lead teacher, specialists, coaches, or supervisors. Each facilitator is assigned a core subject in the first and a noncore subject in the second category. For instance, one administrator may be assigned to math and world languages; these two departments meet (separately) in nearby rooms.

Next, you set the stage to execute a successful faculty PLC. Google Forms are a free and easily accessible method for gathering information quickly and efficiently. Before a meeting, e-mail the Google Form to faculty members. Consider three to four areas of focus to offer as menu options for faculty to vote on. These may be school-, district-, or department-specific, or they may be all of these. Allow faculty to choose among options that they are focused on to accomplish. This may include refining their common assessments, building on their own professional development plan, examining student data, and other unique, creative options.

Departmentally, the most popular topic selected will be the topic that month. If there is a tie, the department decides what to do. This is an extremely democratic process that empowers faculty; they own this, and they make effective use of their time on their professional development topics.

You may utilize as one of the selected topics, a 20 percent time. Have you heard about Google's "20 percent time" policy, where the company offered staff the option to work on a topic of their own choice on the fifth day of the week? What resulted was a fourfold success rate of ideas, or 20 percent time providing 80 percent of their ideas/achievements! If this can work at Google, why not in schools? Offering this option warrants one requirement: The performer (team or department) must produce a result related to student achievement. That's it. This can be one of the most well-received and—you guessed it—performance-generating PLCs!

What Happens in the PLC

In the PLC, teachers report to their department-based locations. An assigned secretary and timekeeper takes attendance and submits a narrative Google Form with any relevant data while keeping the department on task. Meanwhile, the administrator/coach rotates between his or her two departments. This may sound challenging, but remember, this is teacher empowered and faculty led. Occasional questions about district regulations or helping facilitate access to something are typically all the administrator needs to handle.

At the monthly PLC meetings, faculty move toward a common goal. Teachers who were at the seat closest to the door in the big auditorium-type faculty meeting of old were found to be staying ten to fifteen minutes *after* the meeting to finish a task, walking out smiling, slapping each other's backs, and feeling accomplished. No more tired, disconnected, or absent teachers. That's progress!

It is important to recognize that getting a faculty into flow with an unfaculty meeting takes time, a culture change, and trust building. Do this by tinkering. For instance, the model described here added the FedEx Day when faculty reported the other topics were not relevant to them. They moved locations for convenience. All these little tweaks allowed the faculty and leadership to refine their faculty meetings into a powerhouse model for the district and state. Flipping the focus, work, and empowerment leads to the most effective method for functional, interactive professional learning. When a team is on a roll, it feels so much easier—and it is.

Departments can join each other for cross-curricular meetings, too. This may occur a few times a year and offers an interesting view into shared experiences, especially about students.

The question most often asked about how to implement a similar model is how to manage the minutiae, the intermittent mandates that must be communicated to faculty. When necessary and you still need to present information, use a screencasting resource such as Loom, a free video recorder, to present minutiae in no more than ten minutes. Faculty can watch from the comfort of their own meeting location and then jump right into their PLC without transitional delays.

Online surveys of faculty showed a jump of nearly twice as much satisfaction when the model school switched from traditional faculty meetings to the un-faculty meeting PLC format. Reporting revealed they received adequate professional development time. Previously, more than half reported they did not receive adequate professional development time. [AU: I'm not clear what the change is here—how many reported they received adequate PD time compared with previously?]

Next Step: Edcamp-Style Meetings

Once you have established engaging PLC platforms for meetings, you are ready to embrace Edcamp-style faculty meetings. Teachers share topics of interest and select a theme that they would like to learn and share about. You'll be amazed by the diversity and creativity of topics. Try this to reinvigorate and build collaboration among faculty.

An Edcamp is a participant-driven conference, commonly referred to as an "unconference," for educators. Edcamps are built around community participation and coordination. It is an authentic way to engage your faculty with the same motivation and learning that transcends to professional development that is highly choice driven at the grass roots level of faculty members. Follow these steps to ensure your school based Edcamp is a success:

1. Designate an organizer: This does not have to be an official leader. An organizer can be anyone with respected influence within your school community.
2. Generate topic ideas: Survey your faculty on the topics they are interested in learning about. Next, create a menu of choices that faculty can

select from, based on the survey results and relevant topics. In a one-hour faculty meeting, you could plan two 25-minute sessions. It is recommended to provide space between sessions to allow faculty to transition.
3. Develop a registration process: A simple google form allows registrants to sign up for sessions and follow up with reminders to complete registration by a hard deadline date. Schedule room locations nearby each other because like a conference, faculty will be checking in and out of their selected options in quick fashion.
4. Schedule room locations: Send a list of attendees with room locations to confirm their sign up and directions for where to go and when.
5. Encourage ingenuity for faculty: let your attendees experiment as a group so that they can troubleshoot together at a future meeting. One way is to offer a "how-to" instructional that reinforces what is demonstrated and offer five minutes of Q&A at the end. This also allows faculty to share ideas about how they might use the newly learned concept, important networking opportunities for all.
6. Consider this a continuum: At the end of the final Edcamp session, reinforce the ongoing nature of Edcamps and topics presented, like 1.0 and a 2.0 version. Implement a 3-step process to ensure sequencing exists from one Edcamp session to the next.

- Issue certificates of completion. This is personalized touch.
- Follow up with survey feedback-what went well, what suggestions do you have, what would you like to see at a future session?
- To ensure sequencing, offer follow-up development in future meetings, based on respondents needs and interests.

Empowering faculty with the tools to lead their own professional development is the most effective way to target student achievement and improve faculty attendance. This faculty PLC road map can be replicated in any setting. All you must do is take a chance, so why not?

CHAPTER SUMMARY

1. *How One School Saved Eight School Days.* Without reducing school vacation time or extending the school year, this practical technique increases instructional time for every child and educator in the school. It can be applied under the umbrella of a larger incentive-based positive reinforcement system or as a stand-alone. Everyone can be a winner—students and staff. It helps to support the bond adults and students maintain in a successful learning environment.

2. *MicroPD for a Better Flow in Your School.* This offers the opportunity for faculty to reinvigorate themselves during those lulls in the year or on a day when they most need it. Invigorating the professional spirit of educators has a direct impact on the instructional excellence provided to students. Arranging these professional development sessions in short bursts and preplanned or pop-up times during the year offers schools and educators the chance to reenergize midday, midyear, and beyond.
3. *Setting the Tone at the Schoolhouse Door.* This seems more necessary than ever as external forces are pushing in on our values as diverse, tolerant, and democratic systems. Embracing a well-advertised and prominent declaration of the school's standards makes clear to all who participate in the school community the strong value that all are accepted, embraced, and supported in a community of learners. Accepting anything less is not only unwise, it is wrong and counterproductive to a healthy and productive community of learners, students, staff, and visitors alike.
4. *Trivia Games: Getting Teams to Bond Rather Than Fight.* Leaders—not the players involved—have a responsibility to reverse personality conflict. A strategy like sharing a personally unique, interesting fact about oneself and then having others guess the owner is a quick, effective way to regain momentum when it is so desperately needed. Toxic teams, no matter how talented they are individually, do not gel and this has a negative effect on their performance. Building bonds through short, powerful methods like the folded-paper exercise is not only a wise idea, it helps to effectively manage the synergy of teams in schools.
5. *Creating Flow in Faculty Meetings: The "Un-Faculty" Meeting.* Change the way your faculty view the dreaded faculty meeting by running an un-faculty meeting. Instead of the traditional faculty meeting, in which faculty sit at their lowest energy point in the day in an auditorium, empower and reenergize them by making this meeting relevant, fun, and project based. Consider a popular new conferencing format called Edcamps for your use with faculty, department, grade level or any other district themed meetings. These are grass roots influenced ways to empower faculty to engage in professional development.

Chapter Nine

How to Know If It's All Working or Not, and What to Do about It

Engaging Parents: Embracing Diversity

SUPPORTING STUDENTS IN NEED WITH A UNIQUE APPROACH TO INVOLVE THEIR PARENTS

The best barometers measure data that is available and painfully truthful. One school recognized this, seeing that nearly 70 percent of the students in greatest need also had parents who did not attend parent-teacher conferences. The population with the greatest need for parent-school collaboration had the highest gap. It's no wonder these children were struggling. How do we fix this?

Schools have changed from traditionally homogeneous communities to much more diverse ones. This can be viewed as an advantage, a reflection of the world we live in today, offering a global perspective in a nation known for its diversity. But when change occurs, the adjustment brings challenges, such as a lack of attendance at parent-teacher conferences for students who may most benefit from the collaboration of parent and school.

Parents of at-risk students often don't recognize the value of these communication processes. Others may have communication barriers because they lack a strong command of English. Some parents may bear persistent feelings about their own schooling experiences in a bygone era, which sustains their fear, logical or not, in ways that create obstacles to their attendance at school functions, especially those that reinforce past traumatic experiences. There is a way to alter this perception.

In one school, the population of parents of children with at-risk markers had steadily increased as the school's demographics shifted. What was once only five dozen at-risk students ballooned to nearly two hundred. This population cannot be dismissed as an unreachable fringe.

So how does a school attract a group of parents who are either accustomed to repelling the school's advances or simply unaware of the need to collaborate with the school to help their children's progress? One school decided to abandon the passive, traditional mechanism so often used in schools to invite these parents and instead took a proactive, crafty approach that other schools can easily duplicate.

The first step in this process begins with identifying who your struggling learners are. One way to do this is by running a data analysis using your student software to highlight struggling students, such as those with Ds or Fs. This works well for spring conferences. For fall conferences, keep it simple: Ask the teachers to determine from diagnostics or preassessments and initial performance reviews who these students may be.

Armed with a list of identified students, organize the roster into a spreadsheet. Now you can use the schoolwide communication alert system to reach out to the identified group.

Now that a roster is organized into a spreadsheet, a school-wide communication alert system can be utilized to reach the identified group. A sample communication template is listed in appendix C. This communication positively encourages parents to work with the teachers to support their children by attending a conference set up exclusively for them before scheduling is opened to the full school population.

This preliminary step is important because the parents who have less need for such a conference are often most enthusiastic about scheduling them. Teacher availability quickly forces parents of at-risk students out of the most convenient time slots for parents who are often busy working or already reluctant to attend. This perpetuates the cycle: Struggling students remain at a disadvantage due to a lack of school-parent interaction to overcome the very barrier that set the stage for their struggles in the first place.

When this school called families of identified struggling learners to provide advance access to conference scheduling, a substantial increase in participation—from less than 20 percent to more than 33 percent—was realized. That is a significant improvement.

But the school was not satisfied with what they considered a modest improvement. Therefore, the school leadership took it a step further, with a courtesy follow-up call that was made a day or two later by the school's clerical staff—a nonaggressive, friendly reminder inviting them to schedule in advance. The result? An immediate doubling from 33 percent to 66 percent of identified families confirmed for conferences!

Although those numbers were a significant improvement, they were not enough to know that we provided every opportunity to increase our rate. School leadership began researching the families that still had not scheduled conferences to see if there were any patterns. One that emerged involved communication challenges. This revealed some intriguing obstacles and a remarkably simple way to resolve them: Eliminate the language barrier.

A trend was apparent: Most remaining families spoke English as a second language. Schools that thrive on engaging families from very diverse backgrounds are those that enthusiastically prioritize the delicately developed trust and collaboration between teachers and families that is founded on mutual respect, a focus on addressing families' needs, and the elimination of a hierarchy in a culture where class and cultural differences do not divide the community but instead are celebrated.

This barrier can be broken by recruiting individuals from the school staff who are fluent in the community's most common second languages. In the case of this school, it was Spanish and Arabic. Creating a team able to communicate in the parents' native language added to the trust that was building between parents and school, and the response rate for these parents of at-risk students jumped from 66 percent to 80 percent. Remember that the initial number was less than 20 percent participation.

At each conference scheduling sequence, recruit staff to help make the calls in various languages. Provide them with a specific script and take the time to emphasize the value of building trust, especially in the early moments of a phone conversation. First impressions are powerful, literally impacting this trust factor—for better or for worse—in the first few seconds.

Take the time to practice the dialogue, considering tone, approach, and impact, regardless of the language. Discuss this approach with native-born speakers on your staff and rely on them to recognize and respect cultural factors that may impede the dialogue. Armed with this technique, the school can set out to combat the final stumbling block.

Breaking the path of persistent resistance, the school implementing this approach broke a barrier—the parents of 90 percent of identified at-risk students scheduled parent-teacher conferences! This accomplishment was remarkable, a greater than 70 percent increase. Recall that just a few years earlier the school was failing miserably, with just 20 percent attendance for this population at conferences. Taking proactive and incremental steps to open effective communication channels was the key difference that marked this massive improvement. The school did not blame the parents or the barriers; instead they proactively attacked the barriers in strategic ways and did so by showing a vested interest and responsibility.

A good skeptic would wonder, *Great, we got all these conferences scheduled—but do parents really show up?* No, not 100 percent of them. But 85 percent of the parents attend their scheduled conferences, which is still a massive increase. Parents are arriving at this school, collaborating with teachers, and breaking barriers, when in the past they would not have even considered attending.

Here, they can see firsthand the caring and supportive environment the teachers and school provide their child. Getting parents in the door is victory number one. Getting them to see this nurturing environment is the second goal, and even greater progress is made at this crucial point of recognition.

School and family partnerships built on trust are the only answer to really moving students' performance forward. Do this by meeting parents where they are. This is a strategic approach, like a game plan drawn up by a great coach and executed by his team, with multiple parts that all must be coordinated in a way that achieves the desired outcome.

This is not rocket science. It is simply practical, patient, and sustained work that is taken through a series of uncomplicated steps, where pride about the "way things have always been done" is cast aside. Do this by getting to the heart of reaching children who need it. Engage your parent community and then watch the collaboration fall into place. This has been seen firsthand when parents begin to have faith in the school as a support system where the relationship is forged for a better, brighter future of promise for all our children.

SURVEYING FOR BETTER FEEDBACK

Another way to take advantage of quick, effective data results that reinforce the best possible methods to make adjustments is to retrieve feedback through survey. It is simple to get quick, helpful survey feedback with the use of modern technology. The question is, what should we ask? There are many resources available online to help you answer this question.

One principal, who began his career at a school that prided itself on being the flagship of the district's union, was welcomed by the retiring principal with a prideful salute to how many grievances she could elicit from the faculty year to year. "My average is four to five grievances a year, sometimes it's higher; it's a bad year if I have less than two," she exclaimed proudly.

The new principal was stunned by this philosophy. After all, he believed in nothing short of a cooperative model and grew up professionally in the district he had just left with a collegial working relationship. Having served as a teacher and then assistant principal, he found that work among colleagues stayed collaborative, even with the bumps in the road, after stepping into the administrative role.

The new principal worked hard to maintain this and believed in its direct impact on the school climate, which in turn helped students succeed. What had he just stepped into? Importantly, this was not all put on the principal. It was a time and place when a tough, perhaps Joe Clark–style of principal was needed for this school. Fortunately for him, times had changed, and the quiet masses of faculty were ready for a fresh outlook.

The union stronghold mentality left this principal with his hands in the air frequently during his first couple of years. He felt himself getting sucked into an us-against-them mentality, at least when it came to contract interpretation—something that can puzzle anyone, as contract language can be poorly written and subsequently poorly interpreted.

Amid this confusion lurked a silent majority, waiting for leadership to help the school turn the corner. He didn't know that until one night when he arrived home exasperated after an antagonistic exchange with union leadership. Years later, at a faculty member's retirement dinner, he recalled that night as a measure of appreciation to her, sharing the note he had received:

> Early on in my leadership at the school, there was still a difficult barrier to break through, one where trust was lacking between leadership and faculty. I was trying really hard to show the staff a different way of leadership—one of collaboration. On one frustrating day when it seemed like the trust barrier was too difficult to break, I was driving home and called my wife to say, "I don't get it, don't they know me for who I am? Can't they see that I'm just a guy who cares about them and how we can work together to help children?" That same night, I received a beautiful e-mail from you. You said to me, "I want you to know that we understand how difficult it is to work around some of the issues at the school. However, do not give up hope. Many of us understand who you are and how you want to make this a better place. Don't ever lose sight of that, because we believe in you." It was that one simple message that got me through a lot of combative and challenging situations.
>
> Today, we have a different school. I owe so much of that to you and for your inspiration not to give up on this great faculty. They just needed time to understand who I was, and you were one of the forerunners to know it would happen. Thank you for your confidence. I will miss you.

This simple and kind act set into motion a cascade of initiatives that started with the principal asking one simple set of questions: What do they need? What do they want? He began to research surveys online and pieced together one such survey (see appendix A) that afforded him the opportunity to gauge an array of issues in less than twenty-five statements. To get a large sampling of staff, he incentivized them: If I receive 100 out of 125 faculty responses, you will get to leave the next faculty meeting ten minutes early. He did not know if this would work until he checked the responses, which lit up his screen. He had responses from 114 faculty!

Time, in fact, became an intriguing reveal of this survey. One particular statement prompted, "Time in the schedule is provided to facilitate collaborative work, collective learning, and shared practices." The first survey year the response to this was just 45 percent agreement. Clearly time was a problem, and something had to be done.

While there were many shifts over the course of this year, the principal collaborated with stakeholders to figure out ways—some rather innovative and risk taking—to improve the environment. Time was not the only issue, but it was significant, and it was improved here by a complete overhaul of the faculty meeting structure. Gone were the days when exhausted teachers were expected to sit for an hour after a busy Monday, thinking about the next day and the week ahead, easily distracted from whatever the principal was aiming to accomplish.

That was the other part of the problem. Up until now, the principal set out to accomplish goals that did not include collaboration from the faculty. If we have learned anything from flipped classrooms and self-regulated learning, we would be wise to embrace this type of personally empowering professional development.

Again using information gleaned from the survey, the principal altered the structure of faculty meetings. They became powerful and energizing professional development learning experiences. Faculty could select their topic from a menu and meet in department or grade-level groups of relevance. Administrivia was presented through screencasts and abridged, stripping away the time lost. In just one year, that "time" prompt improved dramatically from 45 percent agreement to over 89 percent. That number has stood for years.

Surveys require both a thoughtful process for utilizing them and the courage of a leader (or teacher in their classroom) to request unconditional and anonymous feedback. Those fearful of these realities may not be ready, but those who are ready to embrace revitalizing, school-wide change would be wise to adopt both the use of surveys and a process to respond to them. This does not mean you should change everything overnight or that you should take all suggestions literally. Ideas can become hybridized to fit the reality of your school community.

Faculty will still recognize the change, feel heard, and increase their loyalty. The school scenario provided is living proof, and the modified school professional development survey (appendix A) is a model that can be adapted for your school community. Try incorporating this in your school and witness the results: the progress that's made as a result of your efforts.

LITMUS TESTING YOUR OWN MEETINGS

There is a natural bias in the way we participate in professional meetings that may lead us believe the way we work is the right way, or at least the best way we know. Yet there are ways to install a check system that allows us to monitor the fidelity of our professional work that is conducive to self-reflection and growth. Although this can be done at any time of year, if you are preparing for school opening or at any set marker you decide to establish, offer a professional learning community introduction that fosters the foundation for this. Simply ask the team anonymously, via an online form or in written format, the following:

- Questions that elevate a team's well-being #1: How can we count on each other?
- Questions that elevate a team's well-being #2: What behaviors should we adopt that communicate our commitment to each other's success?
- Questions that elevate a team's well-being #3: What behaviors should we avoid?

Discuss the responses openly, exploring a common ground for moving forward toward your goals. These are almost always well-principled and show a pattern that you can agree on as a team. Next, after a period of time, review your team's work on this. For instance, one group of teams at a middle school agreed to reevaluate these after ten weeks, a linear marking period for the school.

Prompt your team to challenge themselves with the following reevaluation of their current status:

- Have we stayed true to your ideals, as professed by the team?
- Is there anything we need to adjust about our goals?
- Do we need to recommit to anything we outlined at the onset of the year?

Setting up principled goals and then using a check system to determine our fidelity to these goals is a great way to get a team back on task. Team members can restart their engines. This in and of itself can have a rekindling effect. Evaluating these goals and determining whether the team is on track or needs to recalibrate can enable these practitioners to get back to the goals set out by the team. This is necessary because all too frequently teams get lost, bogged down in day-to-day challenges, and risk losing sight of the very vision they set out to achieve.

Seeing the forest for the trees with self-regulated reminders is both motivating and safe for teams. This is an effective method for checking to know it is all working. Establishing checkpoints is critical and reinvigorating. Allowing the flexibility to remember that you do not have to be perfect to be remarkable is liberating and helps a team bond when they need it most.

Chapter 9

REVERSING THE DISCIPLINE CYCLE AND IMPROVING SCHOOL CLIMATE

Full disclosure: This is not a small strategy, but it's hugely effective. You'll see the evidence that unrelenting discipline cycles can be overturned, and it's worth sharing here. This strategy is a play on restorative justice, with a twist. The goal is to tackle head-on the disaffected child, lost in the fray and feeling like a persistent inconvenience.

The Restorative Service Program (RSP) can operate as a stand-alone or as part of a larger positive behavior support system. Let's look at some numbers to establish the rationale for this premise. Since this program was adopted, one school's suspension rate has plummeted from 6.4 percent to 1.5 percent of students. That's a fourfold decrease! The bullying rate has also dropped by 70 percent.

This did not happen overnight. In fact, it took several years of sustained, focused direction. Cultural shifts take time, especially in the unique case of this school. Here, the code of conduct previously read like a penal colony: *No running, no spitting, no cursing* was some of the language contained in this code. Alongside these infractions was a menu of discipline procedures. Spitting equaled three days' detention for the first offense, in-school suspension second offense, and so on. Here was the trouble: What middle-school-aged child reading this code wouldn't take it as a dare?

Communicating expectations in the negative and promoting the misbehavior by listing it alongside the consequence is problematic for several reasons, not the least of which is the challenge a school authority is presenting, as if to say, "Oh yeah, come on try it!" One educator at the school remembers that when he was new to the school, he told a running child to slow down; the child turned to him and protested, "I wasn't running!" *Just deny*, that was the mantra.

The school changed the language the next year. This included subtle but powerful shifts to language such as: *Walk safely, be respectful to others, use kind words*. This allowed the school to start from a focus on the positive rather than the reacting to the negative. Additionally, consequences were intentionally broadened for context. Zero tolerance is effective at enforcing compliance but not at relationship building for long-term, sustained success.

The RSP engages a trained faculty member one-on-one with the child to talk about constructive ways to deal with issues that are causing them to get in trouble. The student is guided through an activity, and the adult is encouraged to seize on teachable moments. To remove any bias, the adult is intentionally unfamiliar with the student so they spend the first few minutes building relationships. This prevents accountability bias, such as a teacher who grades a student, which provides a neutral ground for a teacher to stand as a true mentor to the child rather than someone that evaluates the student.

The adult serves exclusively in a mentoring role that is nonpunitive. The relationship is fostered as the child sees the adult in the hall and positive interactions flourish. Best of all, colleagues see this teacher publicly interacting in a positive way with the child, helping to further reverse the perception of the student as a troubled child.

Now that the foundation for building relations has been established, let's explore what happens in the RSP session. The program targets student misbehavior in a nonpunitive way. Students are guided to more beneficial behaviors that enable them to focus on the future and the positive, rather than the past and punishment. See the connection to the revised code of conduct? Next, let us examine the process for RSP:

1. A student exhibits misbehavior. This may result in a bullying investigation recommendation, or it may be due to disrespect toward authority or other inappropriate action that is referred to the school administration.
2. The administrator issues the necessary (if applicable) disciplinary consequences and separately recommends a nonpunitive RSP. The RSP is often in place of discipline, or with reduced disciplinary consequences, as an incentive to gain buy-in from student and parent.
3. A faculty member who does not teach the identified student is assigned to meet with the child during the available/duty period.
4. The faculty member is given a brief summary of the infraction and uses the sample guide and one of the corresponding activities during a period when the student has a non-core subject and the teacher is available.
5. The teacher files the documents the student worked on in an archive.
6. Monthly meetings are held to review these with administration and to make recommended revisions.

More can be found on RSP in appendix B. It is important to recognize how valuable this resource program can be because it offers at-risk children a chance. Still better, the program offers the entire school an opportunity for a culture shift. The statistics shared earlier, while profound, do not show the respectful, tolerant culture that now permeates this community. That changed over time. It is not a perfect school environment, and it shouldn't be. Rather, it is a place where children are safe to learn, to make errors, and to recover with support. That is one more way you know it is all working.

CHAPTER SUMMARY

1. *Supporting Students in Need with a Unique Approach to Involve their Parents.* One of the most important ways to engage parents, especially parents of children with the greatest needs, is through parent-teacher conferences. Some parents resist this; others have language barriers. Use a simple multistep process to find ways to significantly increase the attendance of parents whose children benefit the most from parents and teachers working together.
2. *Surveying for Better Feedback.* Offering anonymous surveys is a great way to find out what is lacking for a faculty, and how to correct areas where it is clear that change is needed. Equally, faculty will feel listened to and empowered when they see the changes they have asked for. This is a dynamic way to get faculty operating on productive professional development that is revitalizing for the entire school.
3. *Litmus Testing Your Own Meetings.* Providing a check system for your own professional learning community meetings is a great way to reaffirm or adjust the goals you set out to accomplish at the beginning of a school year or any set marker in time. It allows teams the safe space to reevaluate and to rekindle where necessary. Allow your team to set goals and then recall the answers to the three questions that prompted those goals so they can revitalize their spirit toward achieving those goals.
4. *Reversing the Discipline Cycle and Improving School Climate.* Evidence supports the adoption of restorative justice programs in schools to reduce the amount of negative consequences students face and to improve the school's climate. One school found a way, using a structured, mentor-based format, to engage at-risk children in ways that focus on the positive and the future, rather than punishment and the past. Consider adapting this to your school community, alongside subtle but significant code of conduct language changes today and you will see the shift in your school's culture.

This section has been revised to avoid rights limitations on a piece I previously authored.

Chapter Ten

Utilizing Nonfaculty Adults to Improve Your School Culture

How to Cut Your Bus Disciplinary Referrals by Two-Thirds

Schools that have adopted the New Jersey version of Positive Behavior In Schools (PBIS) called Positive Behavior Support in Schools (PBSIS) have seen the many benefits of engaging students and staff in this research-based practice (Barrett & Harris, 2018), which allows educators to celebrate the successes of students rather than exhausting our attention on the negative happenings and behaviors in a school.

One of the challenges with any positive behavior support model is a difficulty connecting nonteaching faculty to your program. Yet these are often the most critical staff members in your school and can offer some of the most crucial support, as they are often right in the trenches with the children most in need of this positive support.

Consider this: Students who have been in frequent trouble in school are accustomed to negative attention. Sadly, they determine at some point that this is what they are good at and choose to thrive on this path. Unfortunately, this helps no one, least of all the child in an unending path of decline and punishment. What if we could flip the script?

Solutions to persistent problems move the school climate in the right direction, reduce disciplinary referrals, and tackle bullying incidents. In one school, using nonteaching faculty helped reduce suspensions fourfold and bullying incidents threefold! Something was working there. A look under the hood reveals a willingness to try something different.

PBSIS and programs like it are replicable if school communities and their leaders are patient and sustained in their adoption. Resources are available for free. Part of implementing such a program includes a school-wide identification of problem areas in the school. This should be done through data analysis. Run a report of how frequently incidents happen in various locations and at different times of the day. Determine which areas are highlighted by staff and students and use this as your basis for determination. As mentioned previously, many schools use Google Forms or other free data collection programs to determine school community perceptions. This is where you start. When creating a behavior incentive program, it is important to utilize both faculty and students. This is necessary to heighten buy-in from both; programs with positive incentives will not work without buy-in from both faculty and students.

Survey Says...

When one school surveyed the school community and compared this to its own data, four problem areas emerged:

- Hallways
- Cafeteria
- Stairwells
- Buses

Once the problem areas were identified, the school members and students targeted those areas with increased supervision and an incentive-based model, a proven model for school climate change except for one area: school buses.

Why was this area left unchecked? Bus problems are often the most difficult to address. School administrators and faculty never have direct oversight of school buses. They often struggle with trying to encourage better bus behavior, as in this school, where attempts were made by announcing and promoting this as part of the overall PBSIS program. Administrators boarded buses and tried to change their approach when drivers demanded action on those few persistently challenging students, encouraging positive behavior rather than highlighting negative behavior. Yet despite their best efforts, little change resulted.

Start by Empowering the Drivers

This school community determined to look at bus behavior as their most formidable challenge in an otherwise successful implementation of the PBSIS program. Over the summer, a team of staff members examined research and literature on successful bus behavior programs that could be applied on the school's buses.

The first and most prominent change that needed to take place was allowing bus drivers to assign their own bus seats, rather than having an assistant principal or teacher on duty assign student seats. The reason? This gave drivers some skin in the game, whereas previously they had been passive participants carrying out orders dictated by others. This, the school had determined, was a risk, but why not try? Nothing else had worked.

Even before the school had implemented its PBSIS model with bus drivers, administrators saw an immediate result from giving bus drivers the power to assign seats: an instant 60 percent reduction in student referrals. Why? Because bus drivers were given respect and authority over their buses. This is the same way effective teachers manage their classrooms. Why not give the drivers equal respect and opportunity? While they lack some of the professional training, most can achieve similar results with wise intervention-style techniques.

The school could not deny that among its large fleet of three dozen buses, a few drivers were ineffective managers, just as a few teachers are ineffective managers. What does school leadership do to address teachers who are ineffective classroom managers? They coach them. They provide support, training, and more. Don't bus drivers deserve the same support? Since most drivers seem to manage well on their own, offering support to the few that need it can only help. By granting drivers the authority to assign students their bus seats, this school brought bus drivers into the fold by supporting them with coaching and control.

Next, Provide Additional Support to the Drivers

As previously mentioned, bus drivers are an important part of a school's community, and their influence can have a major impact on how we manage student conduct. Recalling the discussion about a bus driver and how important it was to get everyone on board, when the principal called the transportation supervisor to explain that her drivers were an important part of his PBSIS system and that it was time to bring them on board with support, the supervisor was speechless. Used to hearing nothing but complaints, she thought the principal had officially lost his mind. He asked if there could be a meeting with the bus drivers one morning early in the school year to share the plan.

She wished him good luck, as this was—as characterized by her—a hardened group of blue-collar workers who were used to being blamed for problem behaviors and who viewed administrators as "stuffed shirts." The principal prepared a presentation for the drivers. Here's what happened next.

Among the three dozen drivers, there were doubters, just as there are with teachers when adopting a new program. Yet the principal came prepared, ready to answer questions and patiently explain the purpose.

He showed them research and statistics:

- Drivers who consciously interact with students benefit from better bus behaviors than drivers who are punitive focused. (Bear, 1990; Mayer & Sulzer-Azaroff, 2002; Mayer & Ybarra, 2003)
- Students' behavior is better when they are incentivized to get rewards for following bus rules.
- Like teachers in the classroom, drivers encounter less disruptive behavior when issuing at least three positive comments to students for every negative or punitive statement. (Intervention Central, n.d.)
- Greeting at the door is positive. One study showed improvement from 45 percent to 72 percent in on-task behavior. Positively greeting each student in one way or another improves behavior. (Allday & Pakurar, 2007)

He explained the primal psychology of misbehavior. Behavior serves one of two purposes: first, to get something, such as attention, objects, sensory regulation; or second, to get out of/away from something (escape). Once we understand the function, we can implement interventions. He advised that they institute simple strategies with consistency to make a big difference. Just scolding or disciplining a student with behavior issues sets the stage for a confrontation, one that gives the child attention. This is preferred over no attention, and the negative interchange results in the driver losing control. Also, as with ineffective teachers, in this scenario the driver is doing all the work and the student is getting all the attention. Switch this and reward most good kids demonstrating good behavior instead.

As some drivers questioned the validity of this new program, something quite the opposite of their prior practice, the principal remembered to never argue with this small but loud group of naysayers. They are better equipped to argue, because naysayers do it all day and have lots of practice. Instead, he acknowledged their concern and asked that they just try it: "What do you have to lose?"

The result: Almost every driver asked for extra incentive tickets to be rewarded to students for good behavior, including the naysayers! Don't argue; instead, suggest what is there to lose and present the option, but don't force compliance. Most will jump on board—this is basic psychology. The rest either resist or are eventually persuaded.

Ongoing Success

The school continues annual meetings with bus drivers and makes it clear to the drivers that they are important to the culture of the school and will continue to be supported. The results have been met with overwhelming success: a 67 percent decrease in discipline than before driver-assigned seating and the school's incentive program were implemented. We might think it is a lot to do, but it's a heck of a lot better than encountering constant bus issues, angry drivers, upset parents, and troubled kids.

Minimizing discipline is an investment that positively affects the whole school. Knowing they have the principal's support, drivers are an active part of this school's positive behavior support program. If you have bus discipline problems, try meeting with drivers, giving them support, and being prepared for some of the humor and bonding that results.

CAFETERIA WORKERS

Most schools have a self-contained cafeteria to feed the masses of students at lunch and, increasingly, also for breakfast. Staff supporting the nutritional needs of students often face the same challenges as bus drivers: Students arrive at their doorstep in a less structured, nonacademic environment and perceive different standards. This often fosters the likelihood that children will escalate their behaviors, if for no other reason than that they are situated in an academically structured environment for most of the rest of their day.

That is why it is even more significant for nonteaching staff to be both aware of and prepared for the energy level that comes from kids' spreading their wings. By applying simple methods, they can both build relationships with students and reduce disciplinary matters. Rather than fighting the hostility often brought on by students, they can utilize strategies that aid their management of the circumstances and create a more harmonious environment.

Like bus drivers, cafeteria workers and recess aides often have little time to establish rapport with children, and, worse, they may fail to see the need to do so. This is where two strategies work. The first is called the two-minute intervention. This has been popularized by some (McKibben) referring to it as the 2x10 method.

Simply put, the adult spends two dedicated minutes a day for ten straight days strategically and subtly engaging in a positive and constructive relationship-building manner with a child who has behavior challenges. This is organized around getting to know the student and using that knowledge to successfully build a relationship. Given the little time that cafeteria workers have with students and the reality that they typically have less training, this is a useful and simple microstrategy.

The second method, referred to as the one-sentence intervention, is similar. This is more feasible for those flash moments these adults—who are not the student's teacher—have to shift the direction of an interaction. It is important to remember that this may or may not work the first time or two with a child; therefore, it is paramount that staff remain patient and sustain the effort. For instance, a teacher of students with emotional challenges remembers greeting one child each morning for ninety-nine days before finally, on the hundredth day, the student turned and said hello in response.

No one is suggesting you try the one-sentence intervention for a hundred straight days before expecting the desired outcome. The point is that kids who have hard shells are prepared for exchanges to turn south because that's what they are accustomed to. Adults working with these children are amazed when they try it, and the outcome most often flips after a few exchanges.

Using the one-sentence intervention microstrategy means we must attribute value to the statement we are making to the student. This occurs when we reinforce a child's value with positive delivery. Positive delivery enables the adult to reference something that opens a child's ears. Here is an example: "I see that you wore your new sneakers today."

Notice that the person did not say, "I love those sneakers," or "Those sneakers are so big." Statements that include value judgments like this should be avoided. Students, especially the tougher ones, feel judged all day, everywhere, and as a result are hardened to good and positive judgments. Indeed, no matter how you offer that value, it will feel like a judgment—or worse, inauthentic or even insincere.

Simply show that you are noticing the child and recognizing a part of his or her persona, attire, and so on in this unbiased fashion. This has the effect, over time, of allowing children to feel regarded and gives them a sense of both identity and merit. They slowly, but steadily, become more active participants when they feel part of something—and all it took was one sentence, a micromoment of acknowledgement.

SCHOOL RESOURCE OFFICERS AS MENTORS

There are families in which many generations have grown up with a fear of authority. This is unfortunate, and the purpose of this microstrategy is in no way to make a political statement for or against the rationale of this fear. Rather, it is necessary to demonstrate the risk of creating adversarial circumstances in the very places where the opposite should and can be happening.

Many school communities employ retired police officers as school resource officers (SROs), and building security has increased along with the tide of rising concern about protecting students and staff in our school communities. Granted, SROs should be there to serve their primary role: to provide a safe and secure environment for students and staff in the school community. But they can do so much more.

In the 1970s, programs like Scared Straight were employed with some at-risk youth to "scare" these children away from a life of crime and into submission. Students were carted off to prisons on a sort of field trip where prisoners, under the direction of law enforcement, literally instilled in students fear of the hellacious day-to-day conditions in prison. This program was conducted under the pretext of causing these children so much fear of the consequences of this life that they would be intimidated into avoiding illegal behavior.

The idea was to frighten these children into staying clear of ending up in the same circumstances as the prisoners shouting at them. Sounds like a good idea, right? Unfortunately, longitudinal studies demonstrate just how wrong proponents of the program were. This strategy was found to be ineffective and even detrimental long term (Lilienfeld, Lynn, Ruscio, & Beyerstein, 2010, p. 225); children who did not participate in this program were found to be better off.

The problem with Scared Straight and other boot camp–like programs that you might see on television wasn't that law enforcement and prison officials were engaging students; rather, it was *how* they engaged the students. If an authority figure or criminal representative symbolizing what children should not do is intended to scare them into submission, the result is identical to negative reinforcement within schools.

We know that short-term compliance may occur, but in the long term, the result is not positive; this is the reason PBSIS models have become so popular. Positive behavior programs are our best solution for decreasing negative student behaviors because students are rewarded for positive behavior rather than punished for negative. This is simple psychology, and educational leaders would be wise to mirror this in embracing an untapped resource: the SROs increasingly present in our schools.

Mentoring is one of the best scenarios to implement an effective adult-to-student program for building positive relations between students and adults. An excellent model of this resides in the Big Brothers Big Sisters of America program. Children who have a caring adult on their side help them make good decisions and avoid risky behaviors (Dubois, Herrera, & Rivera, 2018, pp. 4–6). Not every child can have access to a Big Brothers Big Sisters program, and it is largely not within their control to choose this option.

Traditionally, big brothers and big sisters serve as role models for children who do not have one or both biological parents in their life. This trend is rising, and while many nontraditional families provide a robust and loving home life, the challenge of children suffering from the negligence that tragically happens in many others remains.

It is apparent that mentoring is a positive experience in a child's life and that many who would benefit from mentors most may fear or pose more negative perceptions of law enforcement. The advantage of fostering mentoring relationships between school resource officers and at-risk youth is twofold. At such an impressionable age as childhood, what better way to reconfigure the beliefs of children than to positively expose them to school resources officers, not as foe but as friend?

There are many avenues to build structures to constructively engage SROs with students. Since these two approaches are offered as microstrategies, keep in mind that alternatives, or even a whole new approach, may be considered as options to exercise. The purpose here is to present viable options that you can use to design your own SRO-mentoring model.

The first example of a model for mentoring that integrates SROs is straightforward: If you already have a mentoring program within your school community, simply allow your SROs to participate in it. Better yet, recruit them, pointing out the benefits of a strong positive relationship between students and adult authority figures.

Often this is an easy sell if SROs are retired police officers who were affiliated with youth law enforcement programs such as Drug Abuse Resistance Education (DARE), which seeks to prevent use of controlled drugs, membership in gangs, and violent behavior in minors. Law enforcement programs and SROs who have worked with these programs recognize their benefits, especially from relationship building with students.

SROs remove potential political barriers since they are typically hired by boards of education rather than sourced through limited grant programs or local law enforcement. Therefore, incorporating them into an existing mentoring program involves less bureaucracy, and even if they were not previously police officers, they still symbolize to children through their uniforms and military command structure that they represent law enforcement.

If a mentoring program does not exist in your school community, why not start a pilot program and incorporate your SROs to be part of it? A strong argument is made throughout this text on the influence of positive adult models for children. This is a hybrid of that argument that you can begin almost immediately and, since it's voluntary, with minimal resources.

A second, somewhat more structured method for engaging SROs in a positive adult-to-student mentor relationship is by incorporating a positive program that engages SROs in a guided one-on-one discussion in lieu of discipline as an option that students and parents may select. This incentivizes students and their families to choose a nonpunitive option over discipline.

This option involves the SRO meeting with the child during a lunch or other unscheduled time in the day and strategically away from a disciplinary location such as a detention or suspension room. A guidance or student services office is a viable substitute. At this session, the SRO follows a script to initiate the relationship-building process, stressing the support offered to the student and the opportunity to participate in a dialogue that focuses on the future rather than the past.

This is a win-win scenario: A child who had doubts about the SRO's intentions leaves feeling supported. Better yet, the SRO often develops a long-term mentoring relationship with the child. The next time they share a hallway and that child may be out of turn, running, cursing, or some other variation of the typical misbehaviors that occur with more challenging students, a simple look of compassion and a reminder can help the child to quickly get back on track.

A high five of encouragement, rather than a suspicious look, when the child is managing his behavior sets a tone within the school that gives students a chance to be the best version of himself. What better way to flip the expected negative consequences? Unravelling hardened perceptions is no easy task, as it takes far longer to unlearn something than it does to learn something new. The most impactful, efficient, and sustainable way to do this is through direct dialogue and relationship building. Body language penetrates negative feelings, and one of our best resources are our fastest-increasing school personnel.

Educators and researchers have long recognized the advantage great teachers possess in how they engage the most troubled children and that this rests significantly on their ability to build strong and lasting relations. Duplicating this with SROs—just like bus drivers and cafeteria workers—is a profoundly substantial, long-term solution to the problems that may exist in a school community founded on a support network that offers positive first impressions of law enforcement for those who can benefit from it the most.

CHAPTER SUMMARY

1. *How to Cut Your Bus Disciplinary Referrals by Two-Thirds.* Engage your bus drivers as part of your larger school behavior management program. Even better, give them power in the relationship—if carefully presented and delivered, you will be impressed with both how quickly they jump on board and how effective most drivers are at embracing this.
2. *Cafeteria Workers.* Like bus drivers, cafeteria workers and aides are often the forgotten resource in the school. Tap this resource and see how your students improve their behavior in the most unstructured settings in the school.
3. *School Resource Officers as Mentors.* With the rising tide of school resources officers in schools, this is a resource that is often untapped. While school resource officers should first serve as supports for the

school to secure a safe environment, they can do so much more. Engage your SROs in establishing positive relations with students who are most suspicious of law enforcement and help reverse negative stereotypes.

Appendix A

Faculty Biannual PLC Survey

Please complete the survey. Your feedback is appreciated as we use it to track our efforts and continue to accomplish our school-wide goals!

Staff are involved in/have accessibility to key information and can take part in change.
- ☐ Strongly Agree
- ☐ Agree
- ☐ Disagree
- ☐ Strongly Disagree

Leadership and decision making are promoted/nurtured among staff without imposition of power and authority.
- ☐ Strongly Agree
- ☐ Agree
- ☐ Disagree
- ☐ Strongly Disagree

The principal incorporates advice from staff, is proactive in supporting needs, and democratically shares responsibility/rewards for actions.
- ☐ Strongly Agree
- ☐ Agree
- ☐ Disagree
- ☐ Strongly Disagree

Staff use multiple data sources to make teaching and learning decisions.

☐ Strongly Agree
☐ Agree
☐ Disagree
☐ Strongly Disagree

A collaborative process exists for developing shared values and visions across staff which support norms that guide decisions about teaching and learning with a focus on students.

☐ Strongly Agree
☐ Agree
☐ Disagree
☐ Strongly Disagree

Decisions are made with alignment to the school's values and visions.

☐ Strongly Agree
☐ Agree
☐ Disagree
☐ Strongly Disagree

School procedures in programs are aligned to vision where stakeholders are involved in creating high expectations and data used to prioritize actions.

☐ Strongly Agree
☐ Agree
☐ Disagree
☐ Strongly Disagree

Staff work together to develop and apply knowledge/skills; a collegial relationship exists to improve where staff search for solutions to student needs.

☐ Strongly Agree
☐ Agree
☐ Disagree
☐ Strongly Disagree

Opportunities in structures exist for collective learning and staff dialogue in ways that reflect diverse ideas where staff learn together and apply this knowledge to problem solve.

☐ Strongly Agree
☐ Agree
☐ Disagree
☐ Strongly Disagree

Professional development focuses on teaching/learning where staff are committed to collaborative enhancement of learning and can analyze data sources to assess instructional practices.

☐ Strongly Agree
☐ Agree
☐ Disagree
☐ Strongly Disagree

Opportunities exist for staff to review student work together and observe peers and provide feedback on instructional practice.

☐ Strongly Agree
☐ Agree
☐ Disagree
☐ Strongly Disagree

Staff collaborate to review student work to improve instruction and guide overall school improvement, apply learning, and share results of practice.

☐ Strongly Agree
☐ Agree
☐ Disagree
☐ Strongly Disagree

Staff informally share ideas and suggestions for student improvement and apply learning to share results of their practice.

☐ Strongly Agree
☐ Agree
☐ Disagree
☐ Strongly Disagree

Caring relationships exist among staff or a culture of trust and respect promotes risks that allow for honest and respectful examination of data to improve student learning.

☐ Strongly Agree

☐ Agree
☐ Disagree
☐ Strongly Disagree

Students in this school generally respond to the positive behavior support in the school's system and there is proof in the school climate.

☐ Strongly Agree
☐ Agree
☐ Disagree
☐ Strongly Disagree

Outstanding achievement is celebrated, where staff exhibited sustained and unified effort to impact change in school culture.

☐ Strongly Agree
☐ Agree
☐ Disagree
☐ Strongly Disagree

There has been a general shift away from teacher-directed lower-level instruction toward higher-level learning opportunities of analysis and evaluation for learners.

☐ Strongly Agree
☐ Agree
☐ Disagree
☐ Strongly Disagree

Parents are well integrated into the school community, are given opportunities through school efforts to communicate at the class and whole-school level, and express satisfaction with these efforts.

☐ Strongly Agree
☐ Agree
☐ Disagree
☐ Strongly Disagree

Time in the schedule is provided to facilitate collaborative work, collective learning, and shared practices.

☐ Strongly Agree
☐ Agree

☐ Disagree
☐ Strongly Disagree

Fiscal resources, materials, and technology are available for professional development in practice.

☐ Strongly Agree
☐ Agree
☐ Disagree
☐ Strongly Disagree

Communication systems provide and promote flow of information across the entire school.

☐ Strongly Agree
☐ Agree
☐ Disagree
☐ Strongly Disagree

The school facility is clean and welcoming where the proximity of grades and department personnel allow ease in collegial collaboration.

☐ Strongly Agree
☐ Agree
☐ Disagree
☐ Strongly Disagree

Data is available and accessible to staff.

☐ Strongly Agree
☐ Agree
☐ Disagree
☐ Strongly Disagree

Appendix B

Restorative Service Program Guidebook

EXECUTIVE SUMMARY OF THE PROGRAM, PLAN, AND PROCESS

A PBSIS restorative intervention program (called restorative service program [RSP]) is a method for addressing student behavior that is not punishment and does not dwell on the past. Instead, it focuses on relationships and the future.

Here is the process:

- A student exhibits misbehavior. This may result in a bullying investigation recommendation, or it may be due to disrespect toward authority or another inappropriate action that is referred to the school administration.
- The administrator issues the necessary (if applicable) disciplinary consequences and separately recommends a nonpunitive RSP.
- A faculty member who does not teach the identified student is assigned to meet with the child during the available/duty period.
- The faculty member is given a brief summary of the infraction and uses the sample guide and one of the corresponding activities during a period when the student has a non-core subject and the teacher is available.
- The teacher files the documents the student worked on in an archive.
- Monthly meetings are held to review these with administration and to make recommended revisions.

Appendix B

GOALS OF THE RESTORATIVE SERVICE PROGRAM

The potential positives of the RSP include:

1. *Providing an immediate response for student's actions.* Consequences are most effective when they are assigned with as little time as possible elapsing between the offense and the discipline. By connecting the consequence to the behavior that we are trying to redirect, students can make a connection that may deter repeated actions.
2. *Minimizing disruption to the learning environment.* One of the biggest problems that many educators see with typical disciplinary actions such as suspensions is the removal of the student from the learning environment, which exacerbates what in many cases is already an issue for the offender. The RSP is offered during school and the RSP administrator makes every attempt to schedule the intervention during non-core academic classes.
3. *Providing a structured method to focus on the future proactively.* Often when discipline is assigned, it is done in a vacuum. A detention or suspension is assigned without any follow-up component that can help an offender recognize his or her actions and learn how to make better future decisions. The structured facilitator's guide and student-centered activities provide an opportunity for student offenders to analyze the motivations behind their actions and offer a framework for students to change their behavior.
4. *Providing an alternative to suspensions.* Suspensions in many cases prove to be ineffective for many reasons, not the least of which is the simple desire of some offenders to be suspended. Students who have committed an offense worthy of disciplinary consequences very often welcome suspension because they are in essence being "rewarded" with missing formalized educational time. The RSP is conducted during school without removal of the student from core academic classes whenever possible.
5. *Encouraging positive relationships with authority figures.* In many cases the students who receive suspensions have a negative association with authority figures such as school personnel. By increasing the opportunity for student offenders to interact with adults in a positively structured environment, they can begin to develop more appropriate relationships, which can provide a resource in the future for times when they may need to ask an adult for help.

Appendix B

STRUCTURE OF THE RSP

The RSP requires someone to administer the intervention. The selection of the person who administers RSP intervention is critical. The more adults that a student can be exposed to and form positive relationships with, the better. We gave the program a name—"BE BRAVE"—that serves as an acronym in order to highlight behaviors that are important to reinforce.

The actual RSP is administered at various times. One of the goals of the RSP is to minimize classroom disruptions. In order to meet this goal, the RSP is often administered during physical education, an elective, or a cycle class. On some occasions, if the infraction is of a serious nature, the student is assigned an administrative detention, which is usually served for a half day in the ISS (in-school suspension) room. This gives the facilitator the scheduling leeway to conduct the intervention when available. The timing of the half-day administrative detention is selected to coincide with the least impactful time of the student's day with regard to core academic classes.

BE BRAVE
(Acronym)
School Name
Restorative Justice Program

Bullying is unacceptable.
Everyone is on the same team.

Be responsible for your actions.
Respect yourself and others.
Ask for help.
Violence is never the answer.
Education is the key to success.

SAMPLE FACILITATOR'S GUIDE

Respect

Date: As necessary
Prerequisites: None
Goal: Student will examine reasons that someone exhibits disrespectful behavior, explain actions, defend answers to the questions provided, and present ways to minimize disrespectful interactions in the future.
Vocabulary Focus: respect, disrespect, self-respect, esteem, deference, character traits.

Resources:

- Vocabulary sheet
- Respect worksheets
- Character traits references (search list of character traits online)

Prompt: Describe the situation for which you have been assigned a restorative justice intervention. *Complete Do Now Sheet.*

Intervention Steps:

1. Collect and review Prompt response.
2. Discuss vocabulary for this activity.
3. Determine specific Respect worksheets to use.
4. Have student complete specific Respect worksheets.
5. Discuss answers to Respect worksheets with student. Focus on reasons for disrespectful behavior.

    a. Lack of self-respect
    b. Inability to moderate behavior

        a. Dislike of character traits in individual
        b. Feeling of "unfairness"
        c. Failure to recognize authority figure

6. Have student defend answers and explain ways to minimize future occurrences.

Follow-up Prompt: How can you keep a similar situation from happening in the future? *Complete Closure Sheet.*
Put this intervention into ACTION!

Writing Prompt
Name: _____ Date: _____
Prompt: Describe the situation for which you have been assigned a restorative justice intervention.

_____
_____
_____
_____
_____
_____
_____

Follow-up Prompt: How can you keep this or a similar situation from happening again? What specific steps can you take to avoid another situation like this?

Respect Vocabulary

Specific Vocabulary for Respect Worksheets

Esteem (v): To have a high opinion of

Deference (n): Submission to the desires, opinions, or judgments of another

Respect (n): A positive feeling of esteem or deference for a person or other entity

Disrespect (n): Lack of respect; rudeness

Self-respect (n): The proper regard for oneself and one's worth as a person

Character traits (n): A characteristic or quality that makes a person or animal different from others.

Activity 1
Name: _____ Date: _____

It's about RESPECT

Respect (n): A positive feeling of esteem or deference for a person or other entity

1. Three people in this school that I respect are:

   a. _____

I respect this person because: _____
_____
_____
_____

b. _____
I respect this person because: _____
_____
_____
_____

c. _____
I respect this person because: _____
_____
_____
_____

2. Three people outside of school I respect are:

a. _____
I respect this person because: _____
_____
_____
_____

b. _____
I respect this person because: _____
_____
_____
_____

c. _____
I respect this person because: _____
_____
_____
_____

3. Look at the list of character traits you found online and pick **three** of the traits that you **respect the most**.

a. _____

b. _____
   c. _____

Look at the list of character traits, pick **three** of the traits that you **like the least**.

   a. _____
   b. _____
   c. _____

4. Who was the person that you were disrespectful to and why?
_____
_____
_____
_____
_____
_____
_____
_____

Activity 2
Name: _____ Date: _____
How can you use lessons learned in assemblies or programs you saw about tolerance and respect to apply to your actions of respect toward others?
a. Look for the best in others:
_____
_____

b. Treat others the way you want to be treated:
_____
_____

c. Choose positive influences:
_____
_____

d. Speak works of kindness:
_____
_____

e. Forgive yourself and others:

_____
_____
_____

                       Activity 3
Name: _____ Date: _____
                      Self-Respect

   a. Look at the character trait list. List three traits that you possess that you think make you worthy of other people's respect.

      a. _____
      b. _____
      c. _____

   b. Look at the character trait list. List three traits that you possess that you think are not worthy of other people's respect.

      a. _____
      b. _____
      c. _____

   c. Let's focus on the traits that are not worthy of respect. What can you do to work on these to minimize their effect on your life?

   _____
   _____
   _____
   _____
   _____

Activity 4
Name:_____ Date: _____
Directions:

   1. Read each of the following quotes.
   2. After each quote summarize what the quote is saying by putting it in your own words.
   3. Write which quote is your favorite and why?

Appendix B

1. "I speak to everyone in the same way, whether he is the garbage man or the president of the university."—Albert Einstein

    In your own words: _____
    _____
    _____
    _____
    _____

2. "Respect yourself and others will respect you."—Confucius

    In your own words: _____
    _____
    _____
    _____
    _____

3. "When people do not respect us we are sharply offended; yet deep down in his private heart no man much respects himself."—Mark Twain

    In your own words: _____
    _____
    _____
    _____
    _____

4. "This is how you start to get respect, by offering something that you have."—Mitch Albom

    In your own words: _____
    _____
    _____
    _____
    _____

5. "Respect your efforts, respect yourself. Self-respect leads to self-discipline. When you have both firmly under your belt, that's real power."—Clint Eastwood

    In your own words: _____
    _____
    _____
    _____

6. "If you want to be respected by others the great thing is to respect yourself. Only by that, only by self-respect will you compel others to respect you."—Fyodor Dostoyevsky

   In your own words: _____

7. "Football is like life, it requires perseverance, hard work, sacrifice, dedication, respect for authority."—Vince Lombardi

   In your own words: _____

8. "If you want to be respected, you must respect yourself."—Anonymous

   In your own words: _____

Which quote is your favorite and why?

Closure Activity

Appendix B 125

Name: _____ Date: _____

Put it into ACTION!

Give at least three examples of how you can show respect in the following areas/situations:

1. In the classroom:

    a. _____
    b. _____
    c. _____

2. In the hallways:

    a. _____
    b. _____
    c. _____

3. In the cafeteria:

    a. _____
    b. _____
    c. _____

4. On the bus:

    a. _____
    b. _____
    c. _____

5. During school events or assemblies:

    a. _____
    b. _____
    c. _____

Appendix C

Sample Communication Template

Good day Parent,

This is _____, the principal of [school name] with an important message about your child's academic progress and scheduling parent-teacher conferences. All parents are receiving a general call from me explaining the scheduling instructions for arranging conferences with their child's teachers. This call is in advance of the general call to all parents because your child's current academic performance suggests there may be a need to help support him or her, due to benefiting from our collaboration with you. Therefore, please call [phone number] between 3:00–7:00 pm on, [date]. You will be informed which classes a conference is recommended for and given priority to schedule with teachers during the week of parent-teacher conferences.

Parent-teacher conferences are [list of dates]. Students will have a half day with lunch on those days.

Please understand that this is specific to your child's performance on current assessments and it is imperative that you arrange this conference in order to collaborate with the teacher to develop a plan to help your child meet with greater success during the remainder of the school year.

Should you have any questions about this request, or your child's performance, please do not hesitate to contact your child's school counselor. In the meantime, please call us on [restate date to call here] so that together, we can help your child be successful during the critical transitional stage of middle school. Again, that number for [date to call restated again] is: [phone number restated]

Thank you.

Bibliography

All Things PLC. (n.d.). "Articles & Research." Retrieved December 30, 2019, from https://www.allthingsplc.info/articles-research

Allday, R. A., & Pakurar, K. (2007). "Effects of Teacher Greetings on Student On-Task Behavior." *Journal of Applied Behavior Analysis*, *40*(2), 317–20. Retrieved December 3, 2019, from https://www.ncbi.nlm.nih.gov/pmc/articles/PMC1885415/

Barrett, N., & Harris, D. N. (2018, October 23). *A Different Approach to Student Behavior: Addressing School Discipline and Socio-Emotional Learning through Positive Behavior Intervention Systems Publications.* Retrieved July 4, 2019, from https://educationresearchalliancenola.org/publications/a-different-approach-to-student-behavior-addressing-school-discipline-and-socio-emotional-learning-through-positive-behavior-intervention-system

Bear, G. G. (1990). "Best Practices in School Discipline." In A. Thomas & J. Grimes (Eds.). *Best Practices in School Psychology—II* (pp. 649–63). Washington, DC: National Association of School Psychologists.

Bergland, C. (2014, September 25). "Moving Your Body Is Good for Your Mind." *Psychology Today*. Retrieved October 30, 2019, from https://www.psychologytoday.com/us/blog/the-athletes-way/201409/moving-your-body-is-good-your-mind

Chang, J. C. S. (2008, February 12). "Why Do Kids Lie?" ABC News. Retrieved December 7, 2019, from https://abcnews.go.com/amp/GMA/story?id=4277319&page=1

Dubois, D., Herrera, C., & Rivera, J. (2018). *Investigation of Long-Term Effects of the Big Brothers Big Sisters Community-Based Mentoring Program: Final Technical Report for OJJDP* (Office of Juvenile Justice and Delinquency Prevention, Document No. 251521). Retrieved from https://www.ncjrs.gov/pdffiles1/ojjdp/grants/251521.pdf

Gaskell, M. (2018, October 11). "We Used Technology to Increase Attendance at PTA Meetings." *eSchool News*. Retrieved February 16, 2020, from https://www.eschoolnews.com/2018/10/11/we-used-technology-to-increase-attendance-at-pta-meetings/

Gaskell, M. (2018, October 25). "Using Technology to Embrace the "Un-Faculty" Meeting." *eSchool News*. Retrieved February 16, 2020, from https://www.eschoolnews.com/2018/10/25/using-technology-to-embrace-the-un-faculty-meeting/

Gaskell, M. (2019, January 15). "One Small, Shy Child Changed My School's Dress Code." *eSchool News*. Retrieved February 16, 2020, from https://www.eschoolnews.com/2019/01/15/one-small-shy-child-changed-my-schools-dress-code

Gaskell, M. (2019, January 22). "How to Cut Your Bus Disciplinary Referrals by 67 Percent." *eSchool News*. Retrieved February 16, 2020, from https://www.eschoolnews.com/2019/01/22/how-to-cut-your-bus-disciplinary-referrals-by-67-percent/

Gaskell, M. (2019, January 31). "Feeling the Midyear Slump? Recharge Your Meetings with MicroPD." *eSchool News*. Retrieved February 16, 2020, from https://www.eschoolnews.com/2019/01/31/feeling-the-midyear-slump-recharge-your-meetings-with-micropd/

Gaskell, M. (2019, February 21). "How to Change Your School Culture on the Cheap." *eSchool News*. Retrieved February 16, 2020, from https://www.eschoolnews.com/2019/02/21/how-to-change-your-school-culture-on-the-cheap/

Harms, W. (2011, January 13). "Writing about Worries Eases Anxiety and Improves Test Performance." *UChicago News*. Retrieved September 13, 2019, from https://news.uchicago.edu/story/writing-about-worries-eases-anxiety-and-improves-test-performance

Herrera, C., DuBois, D. L., & Grossman, J. (2017, April 24). "The Role of Risk." MDRC (formerly Manpower Demonstration Research Corporation). Retrieved October 2, 2019, from https://www.mdrc.org/publication/role-risk

Intervention Central. (n.d.). "School-Wide Strategies for Managing . . . BUS CONDUCT." Retrieved October 21, 2019, from https://www.interventioncentral.org/behavioral-interventions/schoolwide-classroommgmt/school-wide-strategies-managing-bus-conduct

Jensen, E. (2005). "Movement and Learning." In *Teaching with the Brain in Mind*, 2nd ed. Alexandria, VA: Association for Supervision and Curriculum Development. Retrieved December 30, 2019, from http://www.ascd.org/publications/books/104013/chapters/Movement-and-Learning.aspx

Kennelly, L., & Monrad, M. (2007). *Approaches to Dropout Prevention: Heeding Early Warning Signs with Appropriate Interventions*. Washington, DC: National High School Center at the American Institutes for Research. Retrieved September 19, 2019, from http://www.betterhighschools.com/docs/NHSC_ApproachestoDropoutPrevention.pdf

Lambda Legal. (2019, April). *National Day of Silence: The Freedom to Speak (or Not)*. Retrieved December 29, 2019, from https://www.lambdalegal.org/sites/default/files/publications/downloads/2019_day_of_silence_faq.pdf

Lilienfeld, S. O., Lynn, S. J., Ruscio, J., & Beyerstein, B. L. (2010). *50 Great Myths of Popular Psychology: Shattering Widespread Misconceptions about Human Behavior*. Malden, MA: Wiley-Blackwell.

Mayer, G. R., & Sulzer-Azaroff, B. (2002). "Interventions for Vandalism and Aggression." In M. R. Shinn, H. M. Walker, & G. Stoner (Eds.). *Interventions for Academic and Behavior Problems II: Preventive and Remedial Approaches* (pp. 853–83). Bethesda, MD: National Association of School Psychologists.

Mayer, G. R., & Ybarra, W. J. (2003). *Teaching Alternative Behaviors Schoolwide: A Resource Guide to Prevent Discipline Problems*. Los Angeles, CA: Los Angeles County Office of Education. Retrieved October 4, 2005, from http://www.lacoe.edu/DocsForms/20031008084414_TABS.pdf

McCombs, E. (2017, September 5). "Sexist School Dress Codes Are a Problem, and Oregon May Have the Answer." *HuffPost*. Retrieved December 11, 2019, from https://www.huffpost.com/entry/sexist-school-dress-codes-and-the-oregon-now-model_n_59a6cd7ee4b00795c2a318e5

National Day of Silence: The Freedom to Speak (Or Not). (2019, March 1). Retrieved December 9, 2019, from https://www.lambdalegal.org/sites/default/files/publications/downloads/2019_day_of_silence_faq.pdf

National Education Association. (2016, January 5). "Oregon Student Dress Codes" [video]. Retrieved August 11, 2019, from https://www.youtube.com/watch?v=r7G7KXDI4vI&t=5s

Pillay, S. (2016, March 28). "How Simply Moving Benefits Your Mental Health." *Harvard Health Blog*. Retrieved November 22, 2019, from https://www.health.harvard.edu/blog/how-simply-moving-benefits-your-mental-health-201603289350

Index

absenteeism, 84
academic requirements, 61
activism, 38
administrators: challenges for, 2, 4, 65; engagement for, 61; intimidation for, 40; leadership for, 93; live streaming for, 57–58; mediation for, 11; parents and, 6, 7, 12, 21–22, 70; pride for, 22; role modeling by, 44; social media for, 13; teachers and, xv, xvi; threats for, 27–28; transparency by, 29–30; unions and, 69
all calls, 6–7
alternative solutions, 17
anger, 26, 39–40
anxiety: for children, 58–59; freewrite test anxieties, 48–49, 50; movement for, 46–47, 50; parents and, 47–48; summary for, 50–51; from testing, 45–46; test-taking quote of the day for, 49–50, 51; three-minute meditations for, 49, 51
assaults, by students, xvi
at-risk students: behavior of, 24–25; challenges and, 1–2, 3; communication with, 89; data on, 90; difficult situations with, 30–32; discipline with, 73; diversity and, 91; engagement with, 107; identification of, 90; mentoring for, 67; psychology of, 2, 32; solutions for, 91; trauma for, xv, 1–2, 3, 18

authority, 3, 23–24, 44, 104–105

behavior: of at-risk students, 24–25; challenges and, 59; of children, 42; of parents, 29; PBSIS, 99–103, 105; RSP for, 96–97; of students, 30, 31, 39, 61, 69–71, 73–74; suspension, 65
The Blindside (film), 72, 73
bonding, 84
boundaries, 14
budgets, 72
bullying, 69–71, 75
bureaucracy, 13, 75
bus drivers, 69–70, 99–103, 107

cafeteria workers, 103–104, 107
cell phones, 12–15, 19
certification, 65
challenges: for administrators, 2, 4, 65; at-risk students and, 1–2, 3; behavior and, 59; with data, 90; discipline in, 24; in education, xv, 7, 11, 63; with 80/20 principle, 68–69; lying, 42–44; mental health during, 11; one-liners for, 32; with PBSIS, 99; positivity with, 72, 75; practical solutions for, xviii; for principals, 68; psychology of, 12, 64; pushback, 61; rule of 9s for, 35; in school communities, 72; seating restrictions, 46; of trauma, xvi–xvii. *See also* difficult situations

children: anxiety for, 58–59; behavior of, 42; creativity for, 72; development of, 73–74; nurturing environments for, 92; one-liners for, 32; parents and, 14, 43; psychology of, 4, 17, 25, 50, 102, 106–107; role modeling for, 15; schedules for, 14; status quo for, 55; studies on, 43
classrooms, 35, 59
communication: with at-risk students, 89; in conflict, 36; discipline and, 96; languages and, 91; in organizations, 15; professionalism in, 13, 14, 15, 38–39. *See also* cell phones
communities: parents and, 57; PLCs, 84–86; pushback from, 61; religion in, 38; school, 5, 14, 17, 49, 56, 72, 100
concerns, 26–27, 32, 41, 78
conferences, 90
conflict: authority in, 44; communication in, 36; confrontation, 40, 41; defensiveness in, 24; diversity and, 44; in education, 83; positivity in, 44; psychology of, 22–23; rule of 9s in, 37–39
conspiracies, 29–30, 32
conversations, 11–12, 16, 19
counselors, 37, 41, 80
creativity: for children, 72; in education, 64; in problem-solving, 83–84; solutions from, 67–68; un-faculty meetings, 84–86, 88

DARE. *See* Drug Abuse Resistance Education
data: on at-risk students, 90; challenges with, 90; measuring, 89; from surveys, 92–94
defensiveness, 4, 24
demands, 26–27
difficult situations: with at-risk students, 30–32; conspiracies, 29–30; emotions in, 26–27; legal threats, 27–28; one-liners for, 21; silence, 21–23, 32; with staff, 23–24; summary, 32–33; with teachers, 24–26
discipline: with at-risk students, 73; in challenges, 24; communication and, 96; before guidelines, 55–56; mentoring and, 97; minimizing, 103; psychology of, 3, 97; school climate and, 96–97, 98; time and, 78
discussions, 48–49
diversity, 37, 44, 89, 91
dress codes, 54–56, 61
Drug Abuse Resistance Education (DARE), 106

economics, 10–11, 72
Edcamp-style meetings, 86
education: authority in, 3; boundaries in, 14; bureaucracy in, 13; challenges in, xv, 7, 11, 63; conflict in, 83; creativity in, 64; DARE, 106; diversity in, 37, 89; flow in, 77; hierarchies in, 66; humor in, 68, 69, 75; leadership in, 83; politics of, 81; positive outcomes in, 4; pride and, 53–54; PR in, 15; professionalism in, 12; risks in, 37; safety in, 27; special, 31, 83; of students, xvi; for teachers, 80; technology in, 45, 57; texting in, 14; time in, 21, 77, 87–88; transparency in, 6; unions in, 12; Zen Dens in, 58–61
80/20 principle: challenges with, 68–69; leadership with, 64–68; of management, 63–64; politics of, 69–71; pride and, 71–74; summary of, 75
emotions: anger, 26, 39–40; in conversations, 19; in difficult situations, 26–27; frustration, 28, 63–64; of parents, 4–5, 19; persuasion and, 15–16; pride, 16–19; regulation of, 59
engagement: for administrators, 61; with at-risk students, 107; in classrooms, 59; with parents, 89–92, 98; professionalism in, 64
ethics, 27
exercise, xvii, 46
explanations, 6
extrinsic motivation, 11

Facebook, 5
faculty: compliance with, 9; empowering, 87; meetings, 84–86, 88; principals and, 94; students and, 55; un-faculty meetings, 84–86, 88; wellness of, 60;

Zen Dens for, 60. *See also* nonfaculty adults
feedback, 92–94, 98
flow: in education, 77; in faculty meetings, 84–86; MicroPD and, 80–81; in school, 77–79, 81–82; summary of, 87–88; trivia games for, 82–84, 88
freewrites, 48–49, 50
frustration, 28, 63–64

games, 59
gift certificates, 11
goals, 63–64, 80, 95
Google, 85
guidelines, 55–56

hierarchies, 66
homework, 11
humor, 68, 69, 75

identification (IDs), 16–19
immunization, 29–30
incentives, 9–11, 102–103
intimidation, 40
investigations, 15–16, 19

language, 56, 91
leadership: for administrators, 93; in education, 83; with 80/20 principle, 64–68; one-liners in, 23–24; in school, 55; values for, 68–69
legality, 27–28, 38
lesbian, gay, bisexual, transgender, and queer (LGBTQ) youth, 37
litmus testing, 94–95, 98
live streaming, 57–58
loyalty, 29–30, 32
lunch lines, 11
lying, 42–44

management, 63–64, 78
mediation, 11, 49, 51
meetings: Edcamp-style, 86; faculty, 84–86, 88; litmus testing for, 94–95, 98; professionalism in, 23, 94–95; PTA, 56–58, 61; technology for, 57–58; unfaculty, 84–86, 88
#MeToo movement, 55
mental health, xvii–xviii, 11, 45, 46

mentoring, 67, 97, 104–107
microaggressions, 81
MicroPD, 80–81, 88
microstrategies. *See specific topics*
mindfulness, xvii, 49
misinformation, 5–7, 26–27
movement, xvii–xviii, 46–47, 50
music, xviii

National Day of Silence, 37–39
nonfaculty adults: for bus drivers, 99–103, 107; for cafeteria workers, 103–104, 107; principals and, 102–103; for SROs, 104–107; summary of, 107
nonteaching staff, 69–70, 99–104, 107
nurturing environments, 92

one-liners: for challenges, 32; for children, 32; for concerns, 26–27, 32; for difficult situations, 21; in leadership, 23–24; loyalty from, 29–30, 32; with parents, 27–28; by principals, 21–23, 24–26; for silence, 32; by teachers, 30–32, 33
one sentence intervention, 104

parents: administrators and, 6, 7, 12, 21–22, 70; anxiety and, 47–48; behavior of, 29; children and, 14, 43; communities and, 57; conversations with, 16; emotions of, 4–5, 19; engagement with, 89–92, 98; frustration of, 28; one-liners with, 27–28; principals and, 40; psychology of, 4; quick chat interventions with, 4–5; rule of 9s with, 35–36, 42–44; students and, 3, 6–7, 42, 44
parent-teacher association (PTA), 56–58, 61
PBSIS. *See* Positive Behavior Support in Schools
PD. *See* professional development
perceptions, 68
persuasion, 9; cell phones and, 12–15; in conversations, 11–12; emotions and, 15–16; with IDs, 16–19; $6 T-shirt for, 9–11; summary of, 19
PLCs. *See* professional learning communities

policy, 16–17, 56
politics, 66, 69–71, 81, 106
Positive Behavior Support in Schools (PBSIS), 99–103, 105
positivity, 41–42, 44, 72, 75
post-traumatic stress disorder (PTSD), xvii
PR. *See* public relations
practical solutions, xvii, xviii, 99–100
preschool, 72, 73–74
pride: for administrators, 22; education and, 53–54; 80/20 principle and, 71–74; IDs and, 19; of students, 16–19, 82
principals: challenges for, 68; faculty and, 94; nonfaculty adults and, 102–103; one-liners by, 21–23, 24–26; parents and, 40; students and, 3, 18; teachers and, 2, 3, 25, 35–36; unions and, 92–93
prizes, 10, 11
problem-solving: creativity in, 83–84; with one sentence intervention, 104; practical solutions for, xvii, 99–100; for teachers, xvi; with 2X10 method, 103
professional development (PD), 58, 80–81, 88
professionalism: for authority, 23–24; cell phones and, 19; in communication, 13, 14, 15, 38–39; in education, 12; in engagement, 64; ethics and, 27; in meetings, 23, 94–95; in school communities, 17; students and, 46, 53–54
professional learning communities (PLCs), 84–86
protests, 37–39
psychology: of at-risk students, 2, 32; of authority, 104–105; of challenges, 12, 64; of children, 4, 17, 25, 50, 102, 106–107; of compliance, 9; of conflict, 22–23; of defensiveness, 4; of discipline, 3, 97; of incentives, 9–10; of investigations, 15–16; of lying, 42–44; of parents, 4; of positivity, 41–42; of students, 18, 45, 50, 83; of talent, 82; of teachers, 4, 18, 78; of teamwork, 94–95
PTA. *See* parent-teacher association
PTSD. *See* post-traumatic stress disorder
public relations (PR), 15
push. *See* persuasion
pushback, 61

quick chat interventions, 1–7
quote of the day, 49–50, 51

religion, 38, 81–82
Remington typewriters, 17
resources, 38
Restorative Service Program (RSP), 96–97
risks, in education, 37
role modeling, 15, 44
RSP. *See* Restorative Service Program
rule of 9s: with anger, 39–40; for challenges, 35; in conflict, 37–39; with parents, 35–36, 42–44; positivity in, 41–42; summary, 44

safety, 17, 27, 56, 64–65
Scared Straight programs, 105
schedules, for children, 14
school resource officers (SROs), 65, 66–67, 104–107
schools: budgets in, 72; bullying in, 69–71; climate, 96–97, 98; communities, 5, 14, 17, 49, 56, 72, 100; counselors, 37, 41; dress codes in, 54–56, 61; flow in, 77–79, 81–82; leadership in, 55; PBSIS, 99–103, 105; PLCs in, 84–86; policy, 16–17; politics in, 66; requirements for, 29; security in, 65–66, 81–82; values of, 88
seating restrictions, 46
security, 64–66, 81–82
sharing, 53–54
silence, 21–23, 32, 37–39
$6 T-shirt, 9–11, 19
SMART goals, 80
smartphones, 57
social media, 5–7, 13
Socrates, 17
solutions: all calls, 6–7; alternative, 17; for at-risk students, 91; blindside projects for, 71–74; change and, 18; from creativity, 67–68; for demands, 26; explanations, 6; goals and, 95; from mindfulness, 49; practical, xvii, xviii, 99–100; with students, 41; for time, 78–79
special education, 31, 83
SROs. *See* school resource officers

staff: budgets and, 72; difficult situations with, 23–24; nonteaching, 69–70, 99–104; security, 64–65; time for, 40, 93–94

standardized testing, 45–51

students: assaults by, xvi; behavior of, 30, 31, 39, 61, 69–71, 73–74; bonding for, 84; development of, 2; discussions with, 48–49; education of, xvi; exercise for, xvii; faculty and, 55; immunization of, 29–30; loitering by, 18–19; management of, 78; mediation for, 49, 51; mental health of, 45; parents and, 3, 6–7, 42, 44; performance of, 81; pride of, 16–19, 82; principals and, 3, 18; prizes for, 10; professionalism and, 46, 53–54; protests for, 37–39; psychology of, 18, 45, 50, 83; quick chat interventions with, 1–4; safety of, 17; solutions with, 41; SROs and, 65, 66–67, 104–107; supporting, 89–92; teachers and, xv, 2, 12; teamwork for, 82–84; testing for, xvii; time for, 79; trust with, 97; unstructured time with, 10; values of, 56; wellness of, 58–59; Zen Dens for, 59–60. *See also* at-risk students

studies, on children, 43

surveys, 92–94, 98, 100

suspension, 65

teachers: administrators and, xv, xvi; assaults for, xvi; change for, 18; conferences with, 90; counselors and, 41, 80; difficult situations with, 24–26; education for, 80; one-liners by, 30–32, 33; PLCs for, 85–86; principals and, 2, 3, 25, 35–36; problem-solving for, xvi;

psychology of, 4, 18, 78; sharing with, 53–54; students and, xv, 2, 12; wellness of, 81

teamwork, 82–84, 94–95

technology, 45, 47–48, 49, 57–58

testing: anxiety from, 45–46; freewrite test anxieties, 48–49, 50; litmus, 94–95, 98; standardized, 45–51; for students, xvii; test site visitation day, 47–48, 50; test-taking quote of the day, 49–50, 51

texting, 14

threats, 27–28

three-minute meditations, 49, 51

time: concerns with, 78; discipline and, 78; in education, 21, 77, 87–88; solutions for, 78–79; for staff, 40, 93–94; for students, 79; on task, 78; unstructured, 10

transparency, 6, 29–30

trauma, xv, xvi–xvii, 1–2, 3, 18. *See also* post-traumatic stress disorder

trivia games, 82–84, 88

trust, with students, 97

2X10 method, 103

un-faculty meetings, 84–86, 88

unions, 12, 69, 92–93

unstructured time, 10

values, 54, 56, 68–69, 88

violence, xvii–xviii

wellness, 58–61, 62, 81

YouTube, 47–48, 49, 57–58

Zen Dens, 58–61, 62

About the Author

Dr. Michael S. Gaskell is currently the principal of Hammarskjold Middle School, located in East Brunswick, New Jersey, where he has served for the past fourteen years. He began his career as a special educator teaching middle school learners before serving for five years as a middle school assistant principal.

Mike earned his bachelor's degree from Penn State University and has two master's degrees, in special education and school administration, and a doctorate in educational leadership from Northcentral University. He continues to model the pursuit of lifelong learning through staff development at the local, state, and national levels and facilitates learning opportunities for classrooms and students.

Mike has always maintained a strong emphasis on professional learning communities for teachers, who then foster this same learning community with their students. Gone are the days of faculty meetings in the auditorium. Instead you will see lively, engaging content and student-focused meetings, where teachers start with a purpose and end with fulfilling an instructional objective. This is reinforced in his articles published by ASCD (Association for Supervision and Curriculum Development) SmartBrief.

He also serves as a mentor to new principals in other schools and districts across the state. He often uses his experiences to guide his work in leading other principals through the outstanding instructional leadership opportunities he has indulged in at the local, state, and national levels. With a special love for the middle school and challenged child, Mike has written, cowritten, and supported grants that benefit all children, especially those who just need that extra nudge of support.

Mike continues in his work as a middle school principal, working tirelessly to support instructional excellence within his school, his faculty, the community, and most importantly, the children. He knows it's possible to help any child under any circumstance, even the most overwhelming or daunting one, to excel and become the best version of themselves, and therefore he is grateful to have gotten the chance to give back to every child, every underdog.

Mike has utilized his own personal challenges and experiences to help other struggling learners and students understand that you are not what your struggles are. You are what pushes you past your struggles. Therefore, he firmly believes that you should never give up on any child or adult who experiences struggles in their life. In fact, we should celebrate those challenges and be grateful that someone, somewhere, can help them become the best version of themselves. Second chances make a person stronger and even more resilient.

Mike is blessed with what he calls his "three girls." He has been married to his wife, Michele, for more than twenty years and has two daughters, Gabriella, age fifteen, and Danielle, age thirteen. He enjoys being a father and husband and watching his daughters grow into young ladies.

www.ingramcontent.com/pod-product-compliance
Lightning Source LLC
Chambersburg PA
CBHW030141240426
43672CB00005B/222